ISLAM EXPLAINED

ISLAM EXPLAINED

A Short Introduction to
History, Teachings, and Culture

AHMAD RASHID SALIM

ILLUSTRATIONS BY FARIDA ZAMAN

ROCKRIDGE
PRESS

For general information on our other products and services or to obtain technical support, please contact our Customer Care Department within the United States at (866) 744-2665, or outside the United States at (510) 253-0500.

Rockridge Press publishes its books in a variety of electronic and print formats. Some content that appears in print may not be available in electronic books, and vice versa.

Interior and Cover Designer: Linda Snorina
Art Producer: Karen Williams
Editors: Shabnam Sigman and Nora Spiegel
Production Manager: Michael Kay

Illustrations © 2020 Farida Zaman. All other art used under license from Shutterstock.com and iStock.com.

ISBN: Print 978-1-64611-323-1 | eBook 978-1-64611-324-8
R1

ای درون پرور برون آرای

To my parents, Fauzia and Abdul Wahab.

My teachers and du'a goyān.

My beloved family.

Ata janem, for your love and your example.

And to all who are working toward a better today and tomorrow for themselves and for the world.

CONTENTS

Introduction   viii

CHAPTER 1: **Core Beliefs**   1

CHAPTER 2: **The Five Pillars**   29

CHAPTER 3: **Prophet Muhammad
            and Revelation**   57

CHAPTER 4: **The Shi'a-Sunni Split**   77

CHAPTER 5: **Significance of the Qur'an**   89

CHAPTER 6: **Islamic Laws**   105

CHAPTER 7: **Culture and Daily Life**   117

CHAPTER 8: **Relationship to Judaism
            and Christianity**   139

Glossary of Terms   157

Recommended Reading and Resources   160

Index   165

INTRODUCTION

The terms "Islam" and "Muslim" are ubiquitous and yet burdened with countless contradictory interpretations, misrepresentations, and erasures. Historically, the contemporary political climate or zeitgeist tends to determine how Islam is defined and who is given a platform to speak for its almost 2 billion adherents worldwide. The climate of post-9/11 America bears witness to such vilification and misrepresentations of Muslims and other minority groups. What is clear is that dehumanizing, othering, and stereotyping individuals, groups, and religions is rooted in either a lack of access to the given group or a reliance on misinformation and fringe examples. The fact that you are reading this book suggests that you have a curiosity and an open heart to learn and to grow. I pray that the chapters that follow help answer some of your most pressing questions about the foundations of Islam and its teachings.

This book offers a comprehensive, though not exhaustive, survey of Islamic teachings. Each chapter deals with various aspects of Islamic belief, history, and practice. We will also discuss differences in opinion among Muslims as well as Muslim views on other religions. I've attempted to enliven the discussion with not just the surface-level details but also the inner and interior aims of these teachings. I hope this allows you to have a more complete understanding of what these teachings involve, how they are experienced by Muslims, and the spiritual possibilities they offer. The content is informed primarily by Islam's holy scripture, the Qur'an, as well as those narrations that are widely known and align with scholarly considerations. For readers interested in these narrations, the suggested readings will contain the cited narrations in this text. Lastly, a balanced and nuanced reading of history is employed to represent the historical narrative.

My own journey with Islam and Islamic sciences began when I started to read and memorize the Qur'an as a young boy in the beautiful city of Kabul, Afghanistan. I first taught someone to read the Qur'an when I was 12, living in the Bay Area. From that age onward, I have studied different aspects of Islam and Islamic sciences in the context of traditional Islamic learning, as well as in academia. I began to give lectures in Islamic centers and have been leading spiritual services in Oakland, California, for the past five years. I am also a doctoral student at the University of California, Berkeley. My current research primarily focuses on the study of Islam, Persian literature, and their relations to power and poetics.

My journey with Islam has led to opportunities to engage with faith leaders, as well as invitations to speak and teach at other religious institutions, churches, academic institutions, conferences, and television programs, which have allowed me to engage with individuals from all backgrounds, beliefs, and interpretations. I am deeply inspired by these opportunities to use the energy and potential of religion to bring people together in a way that informs, unites, and activates us all to be and do better. We must strive to soften ourselves to the challenges of the human condition and increase our concern for one another—to combat the immense selfishness and despair that have permeated much of the world. For too long, there have been voices vociferously inciting people toward dehumanization and othering. The results of many of these acts and incitements—whether by individuals, groups, or states—have been violence and war. I've experienced, witnessed, and studied the destruction and pain that results from war and the trauma it leaves behind. This trauma is passed on from generation to generation. It's time for a fresh imagination, a purified intention, and vision toward a new reality sustained in knowledge, wisdom, and compassionate grace that enables us to look at one another with the gaze of kindness and humanity. If this book helps move us even one step toward this, then I have, with the grace of God, achieved my intention.

No human endeavor is perfect. Any shortcomings in this work are mine, and any goodness you see in this work is a reflection of your state. I hope this is a work that you read more than once. I thank you for your time and this connection. Wherever you are and whoever you are, may goodness reach you; *walhamdulilah*.

BY THE NUMBERS

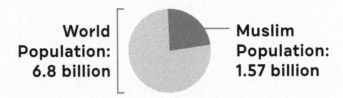

World Population: 6.8 billion | **Muslim Population: 1.57 billion**

Data: Pew Research, 2017

RATE OF GROWTH WORLDWIDE
Estimated percent change in population size, 2015–2060

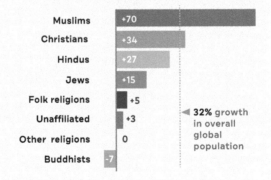

Muslims	+70
Christians	+34
Hindus	+27
Jews	+15
Folk religions	+5
Unaffiliated	+3
Other religions	0
Buddhists	-7

◄ **32%** growth in overall global population

Data: Pew Research, 2017

REGIONAL DISTRIBUTION OF MUSLIMS

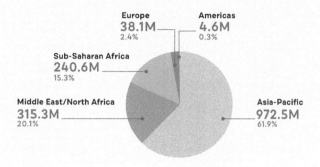

Europe
38.1M
2.4%

Americas
4.6M
0.3%

Sub-Saharan Africa
240.6M
15.3%

Middle East/North Africa
315.3M
20.1%

Asia-Pacific
972.5M
61.9%

Data: Pew Research, 2017

RATE OF GROWTH IN THE UNITED STATES
Number of Muslims in the United States (in millions)

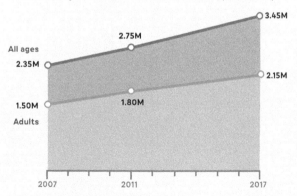

All ages

3.45M

2.75M

2.35M

2.15M

1.50M

1.80M

Adults

2007   2011   2017

Data: Pew Research, 2017

TIME LINE OF THE BRIEF HISTORY OF MUSLIMS IN THE UNITED STATES

Nearly 40,000 Muslims are brought to America as part of the slave trade.

Thomas Jefferson hosts the first iftar for a Tunisian envoy.

First wave of Muslims immigrate to the United States, along with millions of other immigrants.

Early years of America's founding

1805

Early 19th century

Immigration and Naturalization Act passes; and more than 1.1 million Muslims emigrate to the United States before the end of the 20th century.

The first Muslim Students Association is formed (University of Illinois at Urbana-Champaign).

After 1965

1963

Imam Siraj Wahhaj and Warith Deen Mohammed become the first Muslims to offer prayers before the US House of Representatives and the Senate.

After the terrorist attack on September 11, a drastic increase in anti-Muslim incidents is recorded. American Muslims report infringement of their civil liberties following the passage of the Patriot Act.

1991 and 1992

2001

Faiz Shakir becomes the first Muslim-American to manage the campaign of a major presidential candidate (Bernie Sanders).

The first two Muslim-American women are elected to the US Congress (Ilhan Omar and Rashida Tlaib).

Donald Trump signs Executive Order 13769, which suspends immigration to the United States from seven Muslim-majority countries.

2019

2018

2017

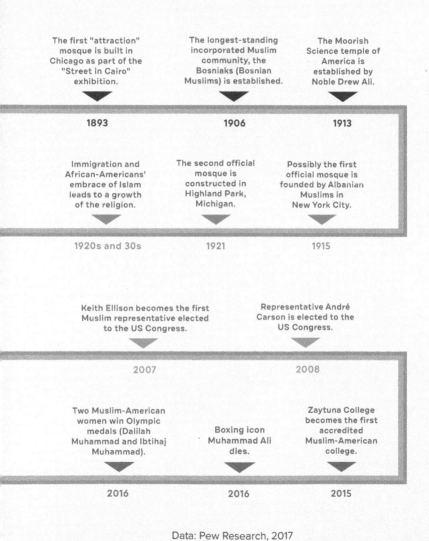

The first "attraction" mosque is built in Chicago as part of the "Street in Cairo" exhibition.

1893

The longest-standing incorporated Muslim community, the Bosniaks (Bosnian Muslims) is established.

1906

The Moorish Science temple of America is established by Noble Drew Ali.

1913

Immigration and African-Americans' embrace of Islam leads to a growth of the religion.

1920s and 30s

The second official mosque is constructed in Highland Park, Michigan.

1921

Possibly the first official mosque is founded by Albanian Muslims in New York City.

1915

Keith Ellison becomes the first Muslim representative elected to the US Congress.

2007

Representative André Carson is elected to the US Congress.

2008

Two Muslim-American women win Olympic medals (Dalilah Muhammad and Ibtihaj Muhammad).

2016

Boxing icon Muhammad Ali dies.

2016

Zaytuna College becomes the first accredited Muslim-American college.

2015

Data: Pew Research, 2017

CHAPTER 1

Core Beliefs

Islam is derived from the Arabic root *s-l-m*, which contains the meanings of peace, serenity, submission, and surrender. Islam means surrender to peace or submission to the Will of God. Anyone who believes in the religion of Islam is considered a Muslim. Muslims believe that in order to experience and attain peace in this world, one ought to understand and align with the Divine Will. That, in turn, leads to experiencing peace both in the heart and in human interactions. Upon seeing one another, Muslims say *"as-Salamo 'alaikom"* (peace be upon you). Islam's holy book, the Qur'an, professes one of the names of God to be *as-Salaam* (the Source of Peace). Muslims consider Islam to be a complete way of life—one that informs, shapes, and permeates their daily life and worldview. This chapter will introduce some of the core aspects of Islamic belief related to God, prophets, the Day of Judgment, and human actions. I will address such questions as: Who do Muslims consider as the Divine? Do Muslims believe that there were many prophets? What happens after death? What is considered a sin?

One God

Islam is one of the world's monotheistic religions. Until the twentieth century, it was common practice in Europe and the United States to refer to Islam as "Mohammedan" and Muslims as "Mohammedans." The use of those terms confused the importance of Prophet Muhammad in Islam and elevated his role to the forefront of what it means to be Muslim, in a way erroneously equating Muhammad to God. Islamic teachings do not elevate Muhammad in this way. The use of those terms to describe Islam and Muslims is now widely rejected. Islamic teachings affirm the need to worship only God and avoid associating any equal or partner or deity with or alongside God.

GOD IN ISLAM

The most essential facet of Islamic teachings centers on the unique Oneness of God. For Muslims, this principle, referred to as *tawhid*, is the heart and spirit of Islam. The Qur'an refers to

God as Allah. Muslims do not consider Allah to be a different deity, or a deity among other gods, unique only to Muslims. Rather, Islam believes that there is only one God. The first portion of the Islamic testimony of faith centers on the statement, "There is no god but God."

Allah, according to Islam, is unique—without similarity to any person, thing, or power—and beyond the limitations of body, space, time, need, or contingency. God is neither male nor female, since neither physical form nor body is associated with God in Islam. This is important to keep in mind when coming across verses in translations of the Qur'an that refer to God with the pronoun "He." Muslims do not make mental associations with a male deity but understand this to be a component of human language. The Arabic language is a gendered language, and *huwa* (he) is the masculine singular pronoun:

"Say He (huwa) is God, the uniquely One" (The Qur'an 112:1)

The verses that follow mention how God is free from need, while all that exists is dependent upon God, the one who is sustainer and provider of all that exists.

God is introduced and known by "signs" and "names." Referred to as the "most beautiful names," the names of God are divided into names of Beauty and Power. These names are in the superlative, such as the Most Merciful, Just, Forgiving, Patient, Kind, Powerful, and the Source of Peace. God is also referred to with the superlatives "Kindness" and "Compassion," as well as "Justice" and "Anger." The superlatives of God are capitalized to signify those qualities are uniquely perfect to God.

Muslims believe that God possesses perfect knowledge and power, knows what is hidden and manifest, and sustains the Heavens and Earth. The opening verse in the Qur'an reads:

In the name of God, the all-Compassionate, the all-Merciful.

The idea of mercy and compassion are essential for understanding God's relation to humanity. God extends mercy, forgiveness, guidance, protection, mental and physical capacity, and life to humanity. Humans have direct access to God through prayer, worship, revelation, and reflection. The fifth verse in the Qur'an's first chapter (*al-Fatiha*—literally, The Opening) reads:

You we worship and You we ask for help.

WORSHIPPING OTHER GODS

Society in pre-Islamic Arabia was predominantly characterized by idol worship and paganism. Idols were considered deities with special and specific powers. Arabs made offerings, sacrifices, and prayers to idols. There were individuals called *hanifs*, which is translated as "one who follows the belief in one God." According to the Qur'an, Abraham, alongside his son Ismail, built the sacred Ka'ba, a cube structure in the city of Mecca. (Abraham and Ismail are both considered important prophets in Islam.) Before it became venerated in Islam, the Ka'ba stored hundreds of deities. It was a ritual site for caravans and pagan travelers, as Mecca was a critical trade and political center for the people of pre-Islamic Arabia, and the Ka'ba anchored Mecca as it still does today.

Being a monotheistic religion, Islamic teachings and Qur'anic verses strongly condemn the worship of idols. The Qur'an belittles idols as false objects made by human hands and questions their usefulness. Islam emphasizes the complete Oneness of God in everything. Since God is considered the True Reality and Being, worship of anything or anyone other than God is considered an illusion, misguided, and an immeasurable wrong. According to Islamic teachings, God is not created, and divinity does not pass to others from God. Islam teaches that God is the First and the Last—this means that God existed before anything else, and that God will exist when everything perishes before the Day of Judgment. There is no room for the worship of anything but God.

As mentioned earlier, God is neither determined nor confined by space, time, measure, growth, loss, or weakness. All of these, according to Islam, are characteristics of God's creation, not of God, the Creator.

CREATION STORY

The Qur'an refers to the creation of Adam and Eve. They were created of the "same essence" (The Qur'an 4:1), perfected by God, and enlivened with spirit. The Qur'an does not state that Eve was created from the rib cage of Adam, but that they were both created from the "same essence." Humankind was created to be the representatives of God on earth (The Qur'an 2:30) and granted knowledge and discernment (The Qur'an 2:31). Angels proceeded to acknowledge Adam and Eve's knowledge, except for one: Iblis (Satan). Although granted access within the realm of angels, Satan is from another category of existence, the Djinn. Satan arrogantly stated that he was better than God's creation and refused God's command.

Adam and Eve were taken from the Garden of Eden as part of their progress on the spiritual and human path. Muslims do not consider the life of this world a punishment or the result of Eve being deceived by Satan. Islam maintains that everyone is born pure and sinless, and Islamic teachings do not contain the idea of original sin. Adam is considered the first in the line of prophets of God. One of the names by which humans are referred to in the Qur'an is "children of Adam."

Islam teaches that humankind was created as an extension of God's mercy and love. However, with time, humankind forgot God and their purpose in life.

The world had to find its way back to God. The Qur'an states that God created humans and granted them life and death as a test to strive for "which of you is best in deeds" (The Qur'an 67:2). Muslims believe that worshipping God awakens humans to their own excellence as the best of God's creation, a key to achieving success in this life and the next.

Angels of God

Angels are one of the categories of God's creation in Islam. They are beings of light, engaged in praise and devotion to God. Just as in Christianity and Judaism, Islam recognizes prominent angels as archangels. The chief archangels in Islam are Gabriel (who brings revelation from God to prophets), Michael (tasked with providing bodies and souls with nourishment), and Azrael (tasked with taking the soul from the body). Angels do not possess any independent power or agency; they perform certain duties only with permission from God. Angels are created of light and they neither go astray nor refuse the command of God. Angels maintain the constant praise and worship of God. As noted in the sidebar "Creation Story," Angels were commanded to affirm the status of Adam as possessing knowledge to which angels did not have access.

ANGELS AND THEIR ROLE IN ISLAM

Angels are an essential component of Islam, through which Muslims come to understand the world in both its tangible and intangible aspects. The belief in angels counts as one of the marks of piety for a Muslim. The Qur'an states:

God bears witness that there is no god but God, and (so do) the angels and those possessed with knowledge, maintaining His creation with justice, there is no god but He, the Mighty, the Wise. **(The Qur'an 3:18)**

Angels are not in competition with humanity. They are special conduits of God's mercy and protection, thereby maintaining a type of accountability in Islamic theology. Angels are intermediaries between the visible, tangible world of humankind and the invisible realm. In Islam, angels are the record keepers for the actions of humankind, good and bad. Some Islamic teachings say that God told the angels to refrain from recording sins and shortcomings for a few hours, so as to allow Muslims to ask for forgiveness and to regret committing such an act. This is a sign of God's extension of mercy to humankind.

In Islam, angels are tasked with delivering protection from certain calamities and harm, as well praying for humanity. The Qur'an states:

And the angels celebrate the praise of their Lord, and pray for forgiveness for beings on earth.
(The Qur'an 42:5)

ANGEL GABRIEL

The most prominent of the angels is Jibreel (Gabriel), who is tasked primarily with the deliverance of revelation from God. The Qur'an states:

> *Gabriel revealed [the scripture of the Qur'an] to your heart [referring to the Prophet Muhammad] by God's permission, confirming that which was [revealed] before it, and a guidance and glad tidings to believers.*
>
> **(The Qur'an 2:97)**

Indeed, Islamic teachings and history mention that it was Gabriel who brought revelation to Muhammad and on many occasions even appeared in human form to further elucidate the message. One such instance is termed the Narration of Gabriel. In this text, it is mentioned that the companions and followers of the Prophet Muhammad were gathered when an illuminated individual entered the gathering, someone whom none of the followers and companions recognized. He asked the Prophet, "Tell me about Islam, oh Muhammad."

The Prophet responded, "Islam means that you should bear witness that there is no god but God and that Muhammad is God's messenger, that you should perform the ritual prayer, give the charitable payment, fast during Ramadan, and make the pilgrimage to the House (Ka'ba) if you are able to go there."

"You have spoken the truth. Now tell me about informed faith (*iman*)," said the angel.

"It is that you believe in God, His angels, His books, His messengers, and the Day of Judgment."

Gabriel said, "You have spoken the truth. Now tell me about beautiful conduct (*ihsan*)."

"It is that you worship God as though you see Him, for even if you don't see Him, [know] that He sees you."

Angels form an important part in Islamic ontology and are considered to be from the world of the nonmaterial or unseen. They are tasked with various roles within this structure, including that of praying for forgiveness for human beings. The categorizations of Islam, iman, and ihsan form an important understanding of the layers and qualifications of spiritual journeying, effort, and realization for Muslims.

The role of angels, and, in particular, Gabriel's role as God's messenger, is essential to the Muslim understanding of Islam and a central part of Islamic identity.

Books of God

Islam believes that God is one and religion is one. Islam is seen as a continuation and culmination of divine revelation, which includes an acceptance of the preceding monotheistic faiths of Judaism and Christianity.

Books of God, according to Islam, are the record of what was revealed to prophets by God. God extended revelation to past prophets like Moses and Jesus, who are considered *major* prophets. The Qur'an refers to previous books of God such as the Psalms of David, the Torah of Moses, and the Gospel of Jesus. What sets the Qur'an apart from other books of God, according to Islamic belief, is that the Qur'an is a revelation after which no other divine book will be revealed. The books of

God all taught belief in the Oneness of God, the doing of good, and the Day of Judgment. Subsequent revelations added onto and clarified previous revelations.

Revelation is a direct and willed act by God and is not considered inspiration. Works that are the result of inspiration are not considered books of God. Although their content can be good and beneficial to the success and refinement of human beings, they are considered outside the realm of divine books.

THE TORAH AND THE BIBLE IN ISLAM

Among the named divine books in the Qur'an are the *Tawraat* (Torah) and *Injeel* (Gospel), revealed to Moses and Jesus, respectively. Interestingly, the Qur'an includes Jews and Christians in a category called "People of the Book," a direct reference to the Islamic belief that divine revelation was sent to them:

> *Truly, We revealed the Torah in which was guidance and light.* **(The Qur'an 5:44)**

> *And we sent after them in their footsteps Isa [Jesus], Son of Maryam [Mary], verifying what was before him of the Tawraat [Torah] and We gave him the Injeel [Gospel] in which was guidance and light.* **(The Qur'an 5:46)**

The above verses illustrate that divine books contain light and guidance and are revealed to prophets. However, a key component of the Islamic teachings on divine books is that many have been lost, forgotten, or changed. Although Islamic teachings emphasize that the Torah was revealed to Moses and the Gospel was revealed to Jesus, they do not consider the Torah and Gospel of today to be the *exact* revelations that were sent to Moses and Jesus. However, it is understood that they still contain aspects of their originally revealed content. More on how Muslims view the Qur'an in relation to past revelations will be discussed in chapter 8.

THE QUR'AN

The Qur'an maintains an active and immediate role in the daily lives of Muslims. For Muslims, the Qur'an is the direct revelation of God to the Prophet Muhammad. In other words, it is understood to be the direct word of God. It is not the inspired words of the Prophet (that is a different category of text, separate from the Qur'an, referred to as hadith, and will be discussed in chapter 6). Muslims read and listen to the chapters and verses of the Qur'an in Arabic, the original language in which it was revealed, and incorporate its teachings into their daily supplications (to humbly beseech and ask God), canonical prayers (the required five daily prayers), and events of joy and sorrow. Many Muslims have memorized the entirety of the Qur'an and subsequently receive the title of *Hafez*: a Muslim who knows the Qur'an by heart.

Included in the Islamic understanding of the Qur'an is that the Qur'an will not be lost, altered, or distorted. Muslims believe that the Qur'an as it is found today is the exact Qur'an that was revealed to the Prophet Muhammad. Muslim belief holds that there is only one version of the Qur'an. Although there are different schools of thought in Islam, they do not have different versions of the Qur'an. In addition to the original Arabic, there are however translations of the Qur'an in all of the major world languages. Given that not all Muslims speak Arabic fluently, they can refer to translations of the Qur'an for further understanding the Arabic verses they are reciting. Recitation of the Qur'an in Arabic is regarded by Muslims to be the true way to speak the verses.

Besides reading the text of the Qur'an, Islamic teachings mention blessings and spiritual bestowal for listening to the recitation of the Qur'an (which tends to be measured and rhythmic). Historically, Qur'anic verses and prayers held a central role in the arts and material culture(s) of Muslims. The Qur'an is considered a conduit of *healing* and *mercy* (The Qur'an 17:82). The healing and mercy refer to guidance, as well as spiritual healing and clarity on the reality of existence.

Prophets of God

The first portion of the Muslim declaration of faith claims

"There is no god but God"

while the second portion states

"and Muhammad is God's servant and messenger."

For Muslims, God sent many prophets to different nations and tribes throughout history. Muslims do not believe that Muhammad is the only prophet of God, rather that he is the final one, with Adam being God's first prophet. Prophets were sent to inform people of the reality of God, their responsibilities to God, and to be examples of a righteous life. Islamic teachings maintain that prophets are divinely appointed, though they are themselves human. Although they are divinely selected and appointed, a prophet's wisdom and excellence is higher than even that of angels.

OVERVIEW OF THE PROPHETS

According to the Qur'an, the prophets who are mentioned by name are not all of the prophets who were sent by God. That number is quite considerable—the common number given is 124,000. Prophets were sent to different people and places. For Muslims, the essential teaching that all these prophets maintained is a belief in the Oneness of God, the Creator of the world. Prophets in the Islamic tradition disavow all alleged partners or equals to God. They proclaim the necessity of doing good and belief in the Day of Judgment. In this context, Islamic teachings consider all prophets to be Muslims, meaning that they all submitted to the Will and the Oneness of God. In other words, the general meaning of Islam is all who have submitted to the Will of God, and the specific framework of Islam includes the formal religion, disseminated by the Prophet Muhammad in the seventh century CE.

MESSENGERS OF GOD

The following list includes the prophets most commonly mentioned in the Qur'an, with the Hebrew/Biblical version of their name next to the Arabic version.

QUR'ANIC NAME	JUDEO-CHRISTIAN NAME
ADAM	ADAM
AYYUB	JOB
AL-YASA	ELISHA
IBRAHIM	ABRAHAM
IDRIS	ENOCH
ISHAQ	ISAAC
ISMAIL	ISHMAEL
ILYAS	ELIJAH
DAWUD	DAVID
DHUL-KIFL	EZEKIEL
ZAKARIYA	ZECHARIAH
SULAYMAN	SOLOMON

SHU'AYB	JETHRO
SALEH	SALAH
ISA	JESUS
LUT	LOT
MUHAMMAD	
MUSA	MOSES
NUH	NOAH
HARUN	AARON
HUD	EBER
YAHYA	JOHN THE BAPTIST
YAQUB	JACOB
YUSUF	JOSEPH
YUNUS	JONAH

ROLE OF THE PROPHETS AS MESSENGERS

According to Islamic teachings, God selects prophets not just as righteous believers and exemplified beings but also to extend and invite others to the divine message. The selection of messengers is a divine act and cannot be determined or changed by human beings. As God's messengers, these individuals invite people to believe in the Oneness of God, engage in righteous deeds, and repent and turn away from any aberration from the true path of God. Given that such individuals are tasked with delivering God's message, they are deemed infallible. Thus, God's messengers do not commit any sin and do not fall into temptations, confusions, or contradiction. As a result of the role and the refinement of character that they possess, obedience to them is deemed mandatory. This obedience does not extend to worship since that is reserved only for God, but the commands and words of God's messengers should be obeyed.

The Qur'an mentions:

> And certainly We sent before you (Muhammad) messengers to their people, so they came to them with clear proofs, then We gave the punishment to those who were guilty, and helping the believers is ever incumbent on Us. **(The Qur'an 30: 47)**

According to Islamic teachings, prophets and messengers are human beings themselves; they are not from the categories of angels or demons or any other creation. However, it is also understood that they are not regular human beings; in addition to their role as prophets and messengers, they are spiritually and intellectually perfect. Many verses in the Qur'an admonish humans who deny prophets and reject their message and even those who ridicule them. God's representatives had varying miracles that they employed; however, the display of miracles is not their primary function. Rather, miracles show and guide humans how to strive for and achieve spiritual and ethical refinement.

THE LAST MESSENGER

In Islam, the prophets and messengers held the faithful to account and judged them on the merit of their actions. This reached its culmination in the message and person of Muhammad.

Muslims repeat daily a testimonial prayer that is at the center of their faith: "I bear witness that there is no god but God, and I bear witness that Muhammad is God's servant and messenger." Islamic faith is not complete without surrender to the truth of God's Oneness, as well as the acknowledgment of Muhammad's primacy. Muhammad is both a servant of God and the extension of God's mercy. Islamic spirituality maintains that love for God extends to love for the Prophet.

The uniqueness of Muhammad's prophecy for Muslims is that he is not just another messenger of God, but that he is the Seal of Prophecy—through Muhammad, the role of prophecy is complete. There will be no other prophets. Why do Muslims believe this? Unlike past prophets and messengers who were sent to a specific people or tribe or time, Muhammad's prophecy is universal. The Qur'an says

> And We have not sent you [Muhammad] but as a mercy to the worlds. **(The Qur'an 21:107)**

Muhammad's message and prophecy, it is argued, is for all of creation and for all peoples that follow. His being and message is "mercy." Another verse states:

Surely, We have sent you with the truth as a bearer of good news and as a warner, and you shall not be called upon to answer for the companions of the flaming fire.
(The Qur'an 2:119)

Muslims believe that as God's "mercy to the worlds," Muhammad holds a unique place in the cosmology of existence, and love for the Prophet is itself a spiritual act. Muslims strive to incorporate the words and actions of Muhammad, referred to as the hadith and Sunnah (discussed in further detail in chapter 6) into their daily life. When hearing or saying the name of Muhammad, Muslims say, "Peace be upon him and his family," and when hearing or saying the name of any other prophet, they say, "Peace be upon him/them."

Day of Judgment

Islam considers each individual to be born pure and sinless. However, humankind is not perfect. People have shortcomings, such as forgetfulness of their duty or falling prey to lust and temptation. Islamic teachings emphasize that Muslims are judged according to what they know, rather than all that there is to know. Muslims hold that this aligns with God's justice. The Qur'an maintains a theme of reminding people of God's mercy and forgiveness, but also of God's anger and punishment for those who insist on misguidance and reject the invitation of God. One verse that relates to this idea states:

But as for one who repents after having thus done wrong and makes amends, behold, God will accept repentance: truly, God is much-forgiving, a dispenser of mercy. **(The Qur'an 5:39)**

SIN AND REDEMPTION

The Qur'an refers to people as *al-insan*, which translates literally as "human." According to scholarship, the root of this word carries the meaning of forgetfulness. A prominent facet of being human is to forget. This can naturally impact many different aspects of our lives, such as when we forget to pay a bill or keep an appointment. There are also certain people or events that we forget with the passage of time. Islam holds that the most terrible action of human forgetfulness is the act of forgetting God. For Muslims, this is among the most immediate concerns. Those who forget God are susceptible to contradicting the law and purpose that God has revealed for the world. This revelation is the basis for everything for a moral, lawful, and righteous life. Those who hear and understand the message are then prepared to adhere to it.

Muslims believe that people, in the course of their lives, will have sins and shortcomings. However, if they ask God for forgiveness, they will be forgiven. No individual can carry or be held responsible for the sin of another. The life of the individual is judged in the context of their righteous actions versus their sins and any aberrations that have occurred. Additionally, by increasing good deeds, past sins will be forgiven. Although Islam considers its revelation and message as the completion of religion and thus the final law, the Qur'an does include references to rewards for people of other divine religions. In chapter 2, verse 62, the Qur'an states:

> *Truly, those who believe and those who are Jews and Christians, and Sabians, whoever believes in Allah (God), and the Last Day and do righteous good deeds will have their reward with their Lord, on them shall be no fear, nor shall they grieve.*

Islamic belief holds that the world in which we live is the realm of endeavor and activity. It is these activities which are aligned either with obedience or disobedience to God.

MAJOR SINS

Muslim scholars categorize disobedience toward God, or sin, into major and minor categories. For the sake of clarity, the following will focus on major sins only. Major sins include associating partners with God, injustice, murder, fornication, usury, giving false witness and testimony, losing hope in God's mercy, and a number of other examples.

Islam contends that sin and disobedience influence both the spiritual and ethical-sociopolitical environments. Sins are linked and impact one another. Forgiveness is prominent in Islamic teachings, so it follows that losing hope in God's mercy is considered a major sin.

Islamic law concerns itself with two areas: the rights of God and the rights of people. Thus, for certain sins, forgiveness primarily lies with the people impacted. For example, fornication is among the major sins, but so is the false accusation of someone being a fornicator. In the instance of a false accusation, the accuser must address this wrong with the accused individual and seek their forgiveness, reforming his or her character to refrain from repeating the act, and also ask God for forgiveness and favor in achieving reform.

DEATH

The Qur'an proclaims, "Every soul shall taste death, then to Us you shall be brought back" (The Qur'an 29:57). Muslims believe that this life is a stage of our existence. A famous account of the Prophet Muhammad states, "be in this world as a traveler," while another notes, "the life of this world is the field of action."

Islamic teachings say that physical death is a guarantee of life, but it is not the end of the human being; death is a stage for the soul's movement toward the hereafter. Once an individual departs from the physical realm of this world, and prior to the Day of Judgment, all souls reside in an intermediate world. They will experience comfort or punishment in that intermediate world, but that too will end. Muslims believe that the final reckoning and accounting will be on the Day of Judgment.

JUDGMENT, HEAVEN, AND HELL

Every individual will be brought back to life on the Day of Judgment. Numerous Qur'anic verses mention the refusal of those who disobey and disbelieve in life in the hereafter. One such verse notes, "[And so] he says, 'who could give life to bones that have crumbled to dust?" (The Qur'an: 36:78). Other verses state that God will bring people back to life just as God first gave life to humans or how the dead earth will be brought back to life.

> *Surely, We shall indeed bring the dead back to life; and We shall record whatever [deeds] they have sent ahead, and the traces [of good and evil] which they have left behind: for all things do We take account in a record clear.* **(The Qur'an 36:12)**

Nothing is difficult for God, the verses proclaim, and humans will be re-formed, matching even their original fingerprints. The Day of Judgment is the occasion of complete and final accountability for all humanity. On that day, humans will be asked about their belief or disbelief in God, their actions, their time, their income (if it was justly earned and justly spent), and many other things.

The Qur'an continually mentions that God's justice will be dealt that day and no soul shall be wronged in any way. This follows the belief in God's justice. Although God can forgive sins and disobedience, God is not unjust, even to those who disobeyed. In other words, it is human action alone that creates distance from God's mercy. Anyone who does not repent, reform, or increase their righteous deeds has no one to blame but themselves. In this reckoning, individuals will be held accountable based on the knowledge they possessed. Thus, a scholar is held to greater accountability than someone who is not a scholar, because the scholar knew more and should have maintained greater ethical integrity.

If the sin and wrongs of an individual are greater than their good deeds, they will be sent to Hell, a place of punishment, despair, and agony. Those who committed to a righteous life with greater good deeds than sins will enter Paradise. The Qur'an talks of Paradise as a site of bliss with gardens underneath which rivers flow—a place of eternal pleasure.

Predestination

According to Islamic teachings, no one chose to be born, and we do not choose the duration of our life, our parents, our ethnicity, or our physical features. However, Islamic teachings make a distinction between those and our ability as people to choose our course of action and beliefs. Our course of action in life is understood to be within the realm of choice and personal decision-making. As a result, we will be asked about our decisions on the Day of Judgment. However, for things that were not in our hands or that we did not have control over, humans will not be questioned. Islam does not believe that there is absolute predestination or absolute free will, but that life has areas of both. God has enabled humans with capacity and choice.

DIVINE WILL

In Islam, God is singular, infinite, and all-powerful. Everything in existence comes from God and depends on God for its sustenance and continuation. This concept is known as Divine Will in Islam, just as it is in the other monotheistic faiths. If for a moment God's sustenance and will are withheld, all existence collapses and terminates. Since everything is codependent, God has put everything in its orderly place; a slight disruption or disharmony would be catastrophic. It was Divine Will that brought about the entirety of creation, both the hidden and manifest realms of existence, from atom to Adam. The Qur'an mentions that God is not constrained by any element or thing.

> *His Being alone is such that when He wills a thing to be,*
> *He but says to it, "Be"—and it is.* **(The Qur'an 36:62)**

In addition to God's supreme power to simply say "Be," Muslims believe that Divine Will only seeks justice and good for humankind. Any deviations and difficulties or negative experiences are a result of human disobedience of God, disrupting the harmony of creation and not maintaining justice—an important Divine command for humans in the Qur'an.

> *Surely, God does not wrong [anyone] by as much as*
> *an atom's weight; and if there be a good deed, He will*
> *multiply it, and will bestow out of His grace a mighty*
> *reward.* **(The Qur'an 4:40)**

Divine Will brought about existence and is what actively sustains and nourishes it. The Divine Will manifests in various ways that impact our lives, according to Muslims. Whether it is the nourishment from sunshine, air, water, food, medicine, or technological advances, Muslims consider their manifestations and their beneficence to constitute Divine Will. Any harm or disruption to befall humanity is the result of human failure to obey the commands of God and the maintenance of the ethical system that Islam has constituted. This understanding aids in reading the following verse:

> *Whatever good happens to you is from God; and whatever evil befalls you is from yourself. And We have sent you [Muhammad] as a Messenger to mankind; and God is sufficient as a witness.* **(The Qur'an 4:79)**

MUSLIMS AND FREE WILL

Free will, or the ability of people to choose and act according to their own volition, is accepted in Islamic teachings. As noted in the previous section, Islam adds a caveat: There is no such thing as *absolute* free will. There are certain natural laws as well as aspects of existence that people do not have control over. Each individual is endowed with the very essential ability to discern right from wrong. Messengers are sent to educate and awaken humanity to the full reality of truth and, in turn, disclose to them the objective rule of right and wrong. Equipped with this knowledge, Muslims are then obligated to perform "righteous acts" and "beautiful acts" and to be "conscious of God" (The Qur'an 3:134; 18:7; 59:18).

God-consciousness, or *Taqwa*, is a central tenant of Islamic ethical and spiritual practice. Taqwa means to have a mental and internal system that cautions, is careful, and prevents the individual from committing wrong.

> *O you who believe! Be conscious of God and keep your duty to Him. And let every person look to what he sends for the morrow!*

Remain conscious of God, for God is fully aware of all that you do. **(The Qur'an 59:18)**

Thus, there is accountability for human actions per the verses of the Qur'an, but similarly there are certain things that people do not choose. Muslims are tested by different situations and challenges, and they view these tests as opportunities to turn to God and increase their awareness, ethical integrity, and understanding of the ephemeral nature of this world.

Islam teaches that there is neither complete predestination nor absolute free will; rather, it teaches that humanity is situated between the two. Any person may come across a certain situation that is out of their hands; how they act is their responsibility and is their own choice. Exerting effort and pursuing their moral and material well-being is a responsibility for Muslims. God grants the ability, and humankind bears responsibility.

CHAPTER 2

The Five Pillars

Islam is commonly described by referencing five foundations of the religion, popularly known as the Five Pillars. The origin of this reference is an account attributed to the Prophet Muhammad. The Five Pillars are understood to maintain the structure of religious life for the believer and the community; they are crucially important in Islam, though there are many nuances to their understanding. Islamic law is helpful in clarifying the understanding of the role of the Five Pillars for Muslims. This chapter will introduce the pillars and the central role they play in the lives of Muslims. The Five Pillars touch on various concepts for believers, ranging from theology to personal piety to social obligation. For Muslims, the Five Pillars are the concentrations of their spiritual understanding and practice.

1. SHAHADAH: DECLARATION OF FAITH

 2. SALAT: DAILY PRAYERS

 3. ZAKAT: ALMSGIVING

 4. SAWM: FASTING

 5. HAJJ: PILGRIMAGE

Five Pillars Declaration of Faith

The *shahadah* is the first of the pillars and the most essential pillar. It connects and bestows all the other teachings of Islam. The shahadah translates as Declaration of Faith. It consists of a two-part verbal utterance and captures the entirety of Islamic teaching. It is one of the first things taught to Muslim children, repeated as part of daily prayers by Muslims, and recited by individuals who convert to Islam.

I bear witness that there is no god but God and I bear witness that Muhammad is God's Servant and Messenger.

Through this declaration, Muslims enter into the community of believers (*ummah*). Regardless of different schools of thought, native tongue, or age, Muslims universally utter the same declaration. In subsequent chapters, it will be shown that there are multiple interpretations and schools of thought in Islam, but the *shahadah* remains universally recognized and maintains the three essential facets of Islam from which all other teachings are derived:

- The Oneness of God

- Prophecy and belief in Muhammad as the last messenger

- The Day of Judgment

THE SHAHADAH AND ITS MEANING

At the basic level, the declaration rejects all false deities and polytheism and attests to the central role of Muhammad as someone who has fully submitted to the will of God and is also God's messenger. Servanthood may sound discordant to non-Muslim ears, but according to Islamic teachings, being a servant of God is true freedom. God desires only goodness and shows humans how to perfect their souls and achieve joy and peace. Hence, if one submits and serves only God, they will be guided, preserved, and perfected.

A more specialized understanding of the shahadah could render it as a statement of ultimate truth in an Islamic sense: "*There is no truth but the Truth of God, and Muhammad is God's Perfected Servant and Messenger*." The shahadah literally means to give testimony or to bear witness, and for Muslims this means that they recognize the "Signs of God" in the tangible, manifest world and through worship, contemplation, and effort. Muslims "see" reality as such and become free from "false gods"—both in the form of physical idols as well as corrupting concepts such as greed, envy, lust, power, anger, and so forth.

SIGNIFICANCE OF THE SHAHADAH

The significance of the shahadah is perceived by its daily role in the lives of Muslims. Within the five required daily prayers that Muslims perform, the shahadah is recited nine times. If the declaration is omitted from the required daily prayer, then the prayer is considered incomplete. The shahadah is best understood as the verbal attestation by Muslims that determines and colors their worldview and is the most essential message of Islamic faith. The shahadah cannot be modified in order to remove any part of it.

The recitation of the shahadah cements an individual as a Muslim. No other Muslim can dispute this. As long as someone maintains their commitment to the shahadah, they are considered to be a Muslim. Muslim scholars hold that no one can state that such an individual is not a Muslim unless the individual harbors and professes a belief that is seen as anathema to Islam.

The shahadah is absolutely pivotal to Islam. If a person spends their life as a non-Muslim but on their deathbed realizes the truth of the shahadah and recites it with sincerity (even if in a language other than Arabic), that person will die as a Muslim; all their past sins are forgiven.

The declaration reflects one name of God: *al-Shahid* (the Witness). As God is witness and sees all things, humans must also witness and open their eyes to the reality of existence.

Daily Prayers

Islamic teachings categorize different types of worship and prayer. Although many varied acts are considered worship, such as pursuing knowledge or visiting the sick, prayers are specific and obligatory throughout the day. There are five obligatory prayers, performed at different points of the day. The performance of these canonical prayers includes requirements that deal with both how the prayer must be performed and steps to prepare oneself prior to its start. The preparation includes the washing of different parts of the body via ritual ablution and facing in the direction of the Ka'ba to commence the prayer. This section will expand on the role and meaning of daily prayers for Muslims.

PRAYER IN ISLAM

The second pillar is a defining facet of daily Muslim spiritual activity: prayer. The worship of God is seen as generating awareness within the individual while situating them in the unique realm of God's mercy. The daily prayers, referred to as *salat*, are the most important ritual aspect of a Muslim's spiritual life, according to Islam. Prayer is considered the pillar of spiritual life and, if unsteady or infrequent, it impacts the harmony and stability of spiritual life. When mentioning salat, Qur'anic verses generally include "steadfastness" with it.

The five prayers consist of a varying number of *units*. The shortest prayer is two units and the longer prayers are four units. Each unit involves different physical movements such as standing, bowing, two prostrations, and sitting. Each physical part is accompanied by a verbal formula recited in Arabic. In addition to the length of the prayers—two to four units—the prayers will either be recited aloud or whispered. Each unit must include the recitation of verses from the Qur'an in the original Arabic. Each prayer takes between four to six minutes and can be performed at home, the mosque, outside, or any other place as long as the individual has permission to pray there.

WHY ARE MUSLIMS REQUIRED TO PRAY?

Muslims understand the daily prayers to be an opportunity for direct communication with God and a foundational spiritual exercise that ensures their commitment and guidance in Islam and draws them closer to God's mercy and grace.

Since Muslims believe that God is truly powerful and generous, they regard that all in the world is made possible only by God's permission. Prayer is vital in maintaining submission to the right of God while distinguishing oneself from those who have disobeyed God. The Qur'an is constant in mentioning the responsibility of being steadfast in prayer and sensitizing oneself through it.

> *And [those] who are patient in adversity, seeking the pleasures of their Lord, and keep up prayer and spend (compassionately) out of what We have given them, secretly and openly, and repel evil with good; as for those, they shall have the (eternal heavenly) home.*
>
> **(The Qur'an 13:22)**

WHEN AND HOW TO PRAY

The daily prayers are linked with different stages of a day. The prayers have the following unique times:

FAJR: DAWN PRAYER. TWO UNITS.

DHUHR: NOON PRAYER. FOUR UNITS.

ASR: AFTERNOON PRAYER. FOUR UNITS.

MAGHREB: EVENING PRAYER. THREE UNITS.

ISHA: NIGHT PRAYER. FOUR UNITS.

The times of prayer inform a direct relationship to the environment and the natural world for Muslims, as well as emphasize that one's relationship to God is active throughout the day. In other words, Muslims imagine that the remembrance of God should inform our daily life. In addition to the required prayers, Muslims often pray additional *recommended* units of prayer alongside each required prayer. Not performing the canonical prayers is considered a disobedience of God and sinful; however, not performing the recommended prayers has no penalty; their performance does increase an individual's good deeds and can wash away other sins. Missed prayers can also be performed later, though Muslims understand that prayers should be performed on time as much as possible.

Prior to prayer, Muslims perform a ritual washing—called an ablution. Water is considered both a purifier and a source of God's mercy. According to a saying of the Prophet Muhammad, "Cleanliness is half of faith" (Hadith on Purification, Sahih Muslim 223). For Muslims, this requires purification of their body and the spaces used for prayer. The ritual ablution has a number of required and recommended steps, including:

- Washing the face

- Washing the arms

- Wiping the head

- Wiping the top of the feet to the ankles (some Muslims wash their feet)

Prayer signifies complete humility and submission to God, according to Muslims. It humbles the individual and ego due to the bowing and prostration to God. Muslims, in turn, believe that bowing or prostrating to anything or anyone else would contradict prayer. Lastly, any individual who is limited in mobility can modify the movements of the prayer in line with their ability. For example, if someone is unable to prostrate or get up from the ground, they can perform the movement while sitting on a chair. Regardless of where they are in the world Muslims pray in the direction of the Ka'ba. This is to signify both the centrality of the Ka'ba as Islam's most sacred site but also to indicate unity in the act of worship by all Muslims.

POSTURES DURING PRAYER

STANDING

BOWING

PROSTRATING

SITTING

THE ROLE OF THE MOSQUE

The mosque is a crucial component of the Muslim community. The word *masjid* literally means a place of prostration—the act of placing the forehead on the ground. However, since Muslims can perform their prayers outside of the mosque, the mosque serves as a place not only of worship but also of communal gathering, learning, organization, and support. Muslims are highly encouraged to perform prayers with their congregation at the mosque if they are able to. It is understood that the performance of prayers in community has greater reward than performing them alone. Muslims also perform their prayers at home, university, parks, or at work.

Prior to the start of prayer, mosques will give the call to prayer (*adhan*). It consists of a number of statements rhythmically recited with a melody by an individual. The role of the adhan is to notify individuals of the approaching time of prayer and invite them to pray. In Muslim countries the call is broadcast publicly from mosques and forms one of the aesthetic soundscapes of Muslim society. In cultures where the majority of people are not Muslim, the call to prayer is often not broadcast outside of the mosque. The adhan's lines vocalize the following:

> God is the Greatest;
> There is no god but God;
> Muhammad is the Messenger of God;
> Hasten to Prayer;
> Hasten to Success;
> Hasten to the best of actions;
> God is the Greatest;
> There is no god but God.

INSIDE OF THE MOSQUE

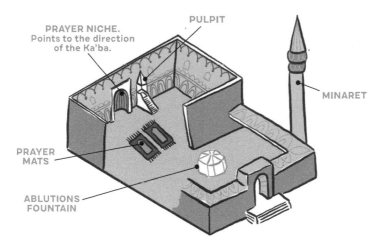

PRAYER NICHE.
Points to the direction
of the Ka'ba.

PULPIT

MINARET

**PRAYER
MATS**

**ABLUTIONS
FOUNTAIN**

MOSQUES AROUND THE WORLD

ISTANBUL, TURKEY

NEW YORK CITY, USA

KULALA LAMPUR, MALAYASIA

ISFAHAN, IRAN

THE SIGNIFICANCE OF FRIDAY

In the Islamic estimation of time and days, it is believed that certain days, hours, and months hold unique spiritual opportunity and grace. The times for daily prayers are such occasions, as is the month of fasting and also the day of Friday. There is a special congregational prayer performed by Muslims on Fridays that takes the place of the noon prayer. Muslims will gather at the mosque to join in. Unlike other prayers, this prayer includes a sermon that is recited by the scholar of the mosque and the sermon is understood to be equivalent to two units of the noon prayer. The sermon has a number of parts, including reminders to be conscious of God, requests for forgiveness for those present, remembrances for those who have passed, and prayers for all who are Muslim. It also refers to socio-ethical-political matters that impact the community and offers guidance and encouragement to overcome flaws in any of these realms. The congregational Friday prayer is understood to be an occasion of unique mercy during which supplications are accepted and shortcomings forgiven. Lastly, it serves as an opportunity for Muslims to see one another and maintain a sense of community and unity. The Qur'an says:

> *O You who have attained informed faith! When the call is made for prayer on Friday, then hasten to the remembrance of God and leave all worldly commerce; that is better for you, if you know.* **(The Qur'an 62:9)**

Almsgiving (Zakat)

The third pillar is a welfare contribution or almsgiving, referred to as *zakat*. The Qur'an has a number of verses that highlight the need for economic stability in society and the need to collectively take care of those who are struggling. Muslims of a comfortable financial and material status are required to donate a portion of their surplus yearly earnings to charity. Zakat has its own detailed method of calculation, as well as a classification of those who can receive the welfare contribution. Zakat is only incumbent upon Muslims who are financially stable and is not required of those who are not financially secure. (These qualifications are defined under Islamic law.)

OVERVIEW OF ZAKAT

Zakat is one of the prominent themes of the Qur'an. It often immediately follows references to prayer:

> *And be steadfast in prayer and pay the purifying charity (zakat); for, whatever good you send ahead for your souls, you will find it with God: For God sees well all that you do.* **(The Qur'an 2:110)**

Zakat is one of the hallmarks of Islam. It cements an understanding of community, charity, and wealth. According to Islamic teachings, the issue of poverty is not one of resource scarcity but rather of wealth not being properly managed and utilized to benefit wider society. Thus, for Muslims, zakat is seen as a religious act that has an immediate impact on social and economic order. Though a full description of zakat under Islamic law is very detailed, it can be summarized. Basically, 2.5 percent of the surplus wealth or property under full ownership of an individual for one year is set aside for use toward charity. The deduction may come from additional savings, certain livestock, jewelry, and other nonessential luxuries.

Zakat is only issued to certain groups. Some of these groups include the needy, the impoverished, and people who are indebted (unless they fell into debt via an activity that is disallowed in Islam such as gambling, alcohol, etc.). It can also be used for building hospitals, mosques, and public works. One of the categories traditionally included was "the freeing of slaves," so zakat funds could also be used to free individuals who were enslaved.

WHY ARE MUSLIMS REQUIRED TO GIVE TO CHARITY?

Zakat is derived from a root word that means to purify or to cleanse. Muslims believe that the Islamic teachings state that charity and welfare-giving purifies a Muslim's monetary earnings. Additionally, it is an article of faith that charitable giving is an action most pleasing to God. By helping others, an individual is blessed and will find good fortune. If someone's wealth is not purified and cleansed through zakat, it becomes a source of disobedience. It is regarded as polluted, a deviation from the correct path, and a source of harm for the individual.

The Qur'an states: "Those who establish prayers and pay the purifying charity (zakat) are sure of the Hereafter" (The Qur'an 27:3).

Complementary to the verses of the Qur'an, the sayings of the Prophet Muhammad emphasize the importance of this contribution as a duty for Muslims and reaffirm its place as a source of blessings. The narrations indicate that by giving zakat, nothing is decreased from that individual's wealth. The zakat ensures their wealth will translate into blessings and that their sustenance will continue. Zakat is either distributed directly by individuals or entrusted to mosques and welfare organizations so that they may distribute it accordingly.

Islamic teachings include sections on zakat for other categories of blessings. For example, the zakat of beauty is modesty. The zakat of knowledge is ensuring that it is taught to and reaches people who will benefit from such knowledge. The zakat of strength and bravery is kindness and doing good.

In addition to zakat, the Qur'an and Islamic teachings refer to a number of other contributions. The most prominent of these is *sadaqah*, defined as voluntary charity that is not confined to any exact calculation like zakat. It's another activity in which Muslims are highly encouraged to take part. Sadaqah can be in the form of giving money or other material possessions, such as land, clothes, or food. Islam encourages individuals to give to causes and activities that will last after they die, believing that good deeds and rewards will continue to be written of the individual long after their death.

THE MEANING OF JIHAD

Jihad means to exert effort, to struggle, or to strive, and it refers to overcoming problems and deficiencies, internal and external. For Muslims, jihad is understood as a spiritual exercise and commitment to conquer the soul (ego/base desires). A famous narration attributed to the Prophet Muhammad states that there are two types of jihad: the Greater Jihad and the Lesser Jihad. The Greater Jihad is to overcome the ego and temptations one faces throughout their days. These may be impatience, stinginess, selfishness, anger, or laziness. One exerts effort and struggles to overcome and subdue such inclinations. It is a jihad to ensure that one performs one's prayers and gives to charity.

The Lesser Jihad is the effort to ensure the safety and protection of one's family, religion, and society. This could be understood as ensuring the physical safety and security of one's community or country. The Lesser Jihad is bound by very detailed requirements under Islamic law and the teachings of Muhammad. A Muslim undertaking the Lesser Jihad is bound to avoid initiating conflict, harming civilians, destroying places of worship, and causing harm to animals and the environment.

As understood by Muslims, jihad does not mean "war" and cannot be used to oppress, harm, or generate injustice. A narration of the Prophet states, "The supreme jihad is of the one who rises in the morning with the intention to not harm anyone." One of the tragedies of the modern world is the misinformation and abuse of the term to mean "war" or "holy war." Terrorist groups often utilize the term to assign a religious facade to their acts. It is worth noting that the largest victims of terrorism are Muslim civilians. Islamic teachings are clear in their rejection of injustice and terrorism, and jihad does not mean "holy war."

Fasting

The fourth pillar is the fast during the month of Ramadan. The Islamic calendar is a lunar calendar—not a solar calendar—so each year the start of Ramadan changes on the Gregorian calendar. Therefore, during a lifetime, a Muslim will fast in each season and each month. Muslims believe that the month of Ramadan is the time in which the first Qur'anic verses were revealed to the Prophet Muhammad. Muslims spend the duration of the day avoiding food, drinks, and sex. Depending on the season, or region of the world, this may vary from 11 to 16 hours. Ramadan is a month of spiritual immersion, reflection, community, and generosity for Muslims. Once it is time to break their fast, Muslims do so by inviting family and friends over, and they spend time in community at mosques for prayers, reading the Qur'an, lectures, and supplications.

OVERVIEW OF FASTING DURING RAMADAN

Muslims view the month of Ramadan as the best of months. It is seen as a time when God's mercy, forgiveness, and grace are most concentrated. The aim of the Ramadan fast is God-consciousness. By refraining from food and drink, one shifts from the consumption of food and satiating the senses toward an inward realm and focus, allowing one to devote oneself only to God. Muslims cite a narration of the Prophet that says each breath of the individual fasting is counted as praise of God, and acts carry rewards proportionately higher than in other months. Muslims must make the intention of fasting—this can be verbal or nonverbal.

Muslims refrain from consuming all food, drink (including water), smoking, and engaging in sexual activity from dawn prayer to a short period after sunset. (Islam only allows intimacy via a religiously sanctioned process.) In preparation, Muslims generally rise before dawn prayers to consume food and drink. Islamic teachings excuse a number of individuals from the fast of Ramadan. They include children; people who are ill; women who are pregnant, nursing, or menstruating; the elderly; and travelers. Moreover, if someone physically cannot fast due to the need to take required daily medications, then that individual is not required to fast. If someone misses a fast due to sickness, they are obligated to make up the missed days when they heal; those who are excused from fasting due to old age or other considerations are to provide food to the poor and needy. Intentionally not fasting is considered sinful. The end of the month of Ramadan is marked by one of the major holidays in Islam, Eid al-Fitr, "festival of the breaking of the fast." It is marked with special congregational prayer at the mosque. To celebrate Eid, Muslims visit relatives and friends, prepare special sweets and treats, wear new clothes, and give money to children.

WHY ARE MUSLIMS REQUIRED TO FAST?

The Qur'an states:

> *It was in the month of Ramadan that the Qur'an was revealed as guidance for mankind, clear messages giving guidance and distinguishing between right and wrong. So any one of you who is present that month should fast, and anyone who is ill or on a journey should make up for the lost days by fasting on other days later. God wants ease for you, not hardship. He wants you to complete the prescribed period and to glorify Him for having guided you, so that you may be thankful.* **(The Qur'an 2:185)**

The fast of Ramadan is considered a complete spiritual act and renewal. By fasting, Muslims believe they are conforming to God's command and sensitizing themselves to the plight of the poor and needy—those who cannot eat or drink whenever they desire. Moreover, by refraining from satisfying their appetites, fasting Muslims center themselves and increase reflection to count their blessings. Muslims believe that the individual who turns inward and analyzes their life will find areas for improvement, correction, blessings, and a renewed commitment to the spiritual path. Fasting Muslims are also encouraged to keep their eyes, ears, tongue, and mind from anything unbecoming, such as backbiting, lies, or a lustful gaze.

The Qur'an is central to the month of Ramadan. Muslims spend time reading, discussing, and listening to the Qur'an. Many complete a reading of the entire Qur'an during the month. Additionally, the last 10 nights of the month are times of increased spiritual effort and concentration. One of the last 10 nights is considered to be Laylatul Qadr (the Night of Power or Excellence). It is also the occasion of the anniversary of the first Qur'anic verses being revealed to the Prophet. Muslims see this night to be better and more spiritually impactful than a thousand months (The Qur'an 97:3)—essentially a lifetime. For this reason, Muslims attempt to spend the entire night until morning prayer in devotion, worship, reflection, and prayer.

Islamic teachings emphasize that Ramadan is a time of forgiveness, hope in God's mercy, strengthening family and communal ties, charity, feeding the needy and poor, and reforming one's character. A narration of the Prophet states that the individual who succeeds in beautifying their character in this month will enter Heaven.

Pilgrimage

The fifth and final pillar is the hajj (spiritual pilgrimage). The hajj is the yearly pilgrimage to sacred sites located in and around the city of Mecca, Saudi Arabia. Islam considers the Ka'ba in Mecca to be the holiest place on earth, so participation in the hajj is viewed as the sacred culmination of a Muslim's spiritual life. Of course, financial and physical constraints limit many Muslims from being able to make the hajj without special help, and even still, many Muslims never make the hajj. For those who are able to afford the pilgrimage, it is incumbent on them to perform the pilgrimage once. No additional pilgrimage is required, but some Muslims perform the pilgrimage to the Ka'ba numerous times in their lives. Muslims believe that the pilgrimage leads to the forgiveness of past sins, purifies the individual, and is a transformational endeavor. The person who completes the journey dedicates their life to increased righteousness and God-consciousness. Moreover, the pilgrimage is seen as a testimony to the global nature of Islam and the oneness of humanity—bringing together individuals of all ethnicities and lands. Thousands of Muslim-Americans make the hajj each year.

OVERVIEW OF THE HAJJ

The hajj is one of the most prominent features of Islam in the global imagination. Each year, it brings together millions of Muslims from all places and walks of life. The hajj takes place during the last month of the Islamic calendar year. There are a number of other pilgrimages that can be made to the Ka'ba that do not count as the hajj.

The pilgrimage consists of a number of requirements. Prior to the start of the hajj, a Muslim must be physically and financially fit enough to be able to complete the pilgrimage. Before they depart, a Muslim pilgrim requests forgiveness from family, friends, and others for any past wrongs. Before the modern era of jet travel, the pilgrimage was an arduous and, at times, even dangerous journey. Despite the vast improvements to international travel today, pilgrims are recommended to complete a will in case they die during the pilgrimage—due to accidents, illness, etc.

The hajj is understood to be a journey toward the mercy and blessings of God. Pilgrims are God's guests and the Ka'ba is the most sanctified place on earth for all Muslims. The hajj consists of a number of acts and has specific obligations, some of which will be discussed in this book.

Muslims view the hajj as a uniquely spiritual experience and an exercise in devotion. Throughout the journey, pilgrims are in constant prayer for themselves, parents, family, and the wider community. After completing his hajj in 1964, Malcolm X changed his confrontational views and realized the possibility of harmonious living and solidarity between peoples of all colors and ethnicities. His peaceful experiences while on hajj stood in stark contrast to the racism and systematic violence that he and other African Americans experienced in everyday life.

Individuals on pilgrimage often act as a liaison for those Muslims not on hajj by praying for them or making specific supplications on their behalf—forgiveness, health, marriage, safety, etc. Muslim pilgrims also visit sites from the life of the Prophet Muhammad, like making the climb to the cave of Hira—where the Prophet Muhammad was said to meditate and pray, having received the first revealed verses of the Qur'an while there in seclusion. (These initial verses are in chapter 96 of the Qur'an.)

A person who completes the hajj is called a haji (male) or hajia (female).

WHY A PILGRIMAGE TO MECCA?

Muslims understand the centrality of the pilgrimage through the Qur'an: "And proclaim to mankind the Hajj" (The Qur'an 22:27). However, why Mecca? The hajj is meant to display an eternal continuity of Mecca as a place for Muslims to commit to God through ritualized prayer at the holy site of the Ka'ba. According to the Qur'an, the prayer of Prophet Abraham for Mecca is as follows:

> *And (remember) when Abraham said, 'My Lord, make this city [Mecca] a place of security and provide its people with fruitful sustenance—such of them as believe in God and the Last Day.* **(The Qur'an 2:126)**

Mecca is a place of history and sanctity for Muslims. It is the place where Islamic prophets engaged in prayer and devotion throughout the ages. Mecca is the Islamic epicenter of belief in the Oneness of God and devotion and loyalty to Islam. Someone who performs the hajj is believed to become a recipient of the supplication of the Prophet Abraham and others who have prayed there.

THE KA'BA AND ITS SIGNIFICANCE IN THE HAJJ

Muslims all over the world pray daily in the direction of the Ka'ba at Mecca. Muslims tie its sanctity and history to the foundations of belief, devotion, and complete submission to God. The Ka'ba is believed to have been built by the Prophet Abraham and his son, the Prophet Ismail. The Qur'an states,

And remember when We assigned for Abraham the site of the (sacred) House [Ka'ba], saying: Do not associate with Me anything and purify my (sacred) House for those who will circumambulate it, and those who will stand before it [in supplication, mediation, longing], and those will be bow down and prostrate themselves [in prayer]. **(The Qur'an 22:26)**

THE HOLY KA'BA

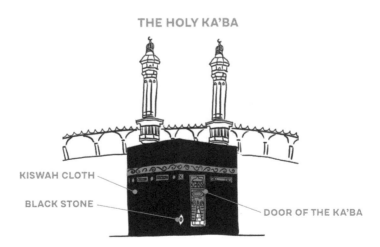

KISWAH CLOTH

BLACK STONE

DOOR OF THE KA'BA

WHAT HAPPENS DURING THE HAJJ

The hajj officially begins when the pilgrim enters the state of *ihram* or sanctity. This can be performed at a number of places just outside of Mecca. Men wear two pieces of white, unstitched cloth, and women dress in loose-fitting, unadorned clothing. The philosophy of the garb is purity, simplicity, and equality. Each stage of hajj combines outer actions with inner dispositions to overcome the major obstacles to spiritual elevation and to draw closer to complete devotion, love, and submission to God. Once in the state of ihram, a number of actions become unlawful for the pilgrim. These include sex, quarrelling, anger, lying, boasting, and needlessly harming all animals.

Once inside Mecca, pilgrims make their way to the Great Mosque, the site of the Ka'ba. Upon entering, pilgrims must perform a circumambulation of the Ka'ba. This walking around the Ka'ba is called *tawaf*. The circumambulation is done seven times. Additional acts, which follow an itinerary, include particular requirements and sites in and around the Ka'ba.

The activities of the hajj occur in the first days of the final month of the Islamic calendar. Once ihram is entered into by the pilgrim, they will spend the remaining days in movement, prayer, reflection, and reading from the Qur'an and books of supplications. The circumambulation occurs around the Ka'ba, then a journey to Mina, followed by moving to the Plain of

Arafat, then onto Muzdalifa, followed by the action of *ramy* or casting stones, and then a return to the Ka'ba. Pilgrims also sacrifice an animal and distribute the meat to the needy and poor.

The act of ramy involves casting stones or pebbles at three obelisks or columns considered to represent the devil, idolatry, and deviation from the path of complete devotion to God. This act is believed to be echoing the Prophet Abraham's act of throwing stones at the devil.

Additionally, Muslims visit the city of Madinah, the site of the Prophet Muhammad's resting place. This is also considered a place of immense spiritual significance where pilgrims have an opportunity to express love and commitment to the Prophet. Pilgrims also visit the resting places of members of the Prophet's family and companions, as well as some historical sites.

The hajj represents the major spiritual pilgrimage for Muslims—often as a result of many years of worship and preparation. Muslims view Mecca and the surrounding holy sites as places of unity and oneness—in the worship of God and of humanity. Each of the actions of the hajj have outer and inner dimensions that tie back to an established spiritual genealogy linked to the Prophet Abraham and other prophets. Lastly, the hajj can be understood to have three facets:

- Journeying from worldly attachments, activities, and preoccupations to God

- Journeying to deeper states of spiritual understanding and consciousness of God—in which the pilgrim increases their reliance on and devotion to God alone and vividly sees the signs of God

- Journeying back to humankind and the social and material world more sanctified and with perfected ethics

CHAPTER 3

Prophet Muhammad and Revelation

According to Islam, prophets are selected by God both as exemplary believers wholly committed to the worship of God and as guides who are entrusted with inviting fellow humans to the path of God. The selection of messengers is a divine act; humans have no say in it. God's prophets invite people to believe in the Oneness of God, engage in righteous deeds, repent, and turn away from anything contrary to the spiritual path. The grand nature of the task assigned to prophets, according to Muslims, requires that prophets be infallible. They commit no sin and do not fall into temptation, confusion, or contradiction. As a result of the role and the refinement of character they possess, obedience to prophets is considered mandatory. This obedience does not extend to worship, since that is reserved only for God, but the commands and words of God's messengers should be obeyed.

Muslims believe in prophecy as a general category of religion and consider admiration for and honoring of prophets as obligatory. Prophecy does have restrictions, and Islamic teachings discuss the notion of false prophets and those who call humankind to deviance under the guise of religion. For Muslims, the first of God's prophets is Adam and the last of God's prophets is Muhammad, who is often referred to as the Seal of the Prophets or the Final Messenger. This chapter will discuss the life of the Prophet Muhammad and the early development of Islam.

Pre-Islam Paganism

The region of Arabia, a vast desert land, was inhabited by various tribes and frequented by caravans and traders in the years prior to Islam's founding in the seventh century CE. The terrain was difficult, and the possibility of cultivating land and livestock was limited by the dry climate. The inhabitants of the land did not share any unified set of beliefs or agreements on religious practices. Tribalism held the most prominent role in the political and cultural lives of Arabia. The prevailing religious environment in Arabia was one of paganistic polytheism. Idol worship was widely practiced. Belief in various deities, often specific to a certain tribe, as well as the spirits of ancestors, was commonplace. The worship of the sun and various planets was also practiced.

Mecca was the most important city in pre-Islamic Arabia. Tribes and caravans from inside and outside Arabia came to Mecca for trade and worship. Mecca was home to a pagan holy place, later recognized in Islam as the Ka'ba. The present structure of the Ka'ba existed during this time, but there were also extant sanctuaries and temples in its vicinity. The early Ka'ba housed hundreds of various deities and idols. Early accounts mention that it included images of Jesus and Mary, as that was home to both Christians and Jews.

Inequality marred the social and economic environment of pre-Islamic Arabia. The rifts prevalent in pre-Islamic Arabian society exacerbated animosities, divisions, and violence between tribes. Muslims refer to the period prior to Islam in Arabia as the period of ignorance, *jahiliyya*, a time when the poor were ignored. Those with power were free to do as they pleased. Islamic sources say that women were considered unworthy and femicide was practiced. There are a number of reasons that are historically presented for this occurrence, such as the belief that girls and women were less valuable than boys, unfavorable and patriarchal norms against women, and poverty (girls were considered to be financial burdens, while boys were viewed as assets).

Wars between various tribes were common, and revenge was expected. Violence between tribes would at times last generations. This tribal conflict, the lack of abundant resources, and the difficult terrain kept Arabia relatively isolated and reduced the risk of territorial expansion into it from regional powers like the Byzantine Empire.

Illiteracy was common in pre-Islamic Arabia, although there are a small number of inscriptions and artifacts associated with the period. Arabs of the time primarily lived in a culture with an oral tradition in which recited poetry served as a source of boast and praise for tribal achievements, remembrance of ancestors, lamenting departure from encampments, romance, and eloquence. The Arabs and their language would journey from the isolation of Arabia to the far corners of the world, thanks in large part to the arrival of a religion by a man named Muhammad.

Life at a Glance

Muhammad was born in Mecca in the year 570 CE, the son of a man named Abdullah. His family was of the Hashemite branch of the Quraysh tribe. Arabia, a society based on tribal affiliations and loyalty, would soon come to know him as the prophet and leader of Muslims. Muhammad's name means "praised." According to the historical accounts of his life, he experienced a number of hardships. His father fell ill and died before Muhammad was born. By the time he reached the age of six, he also lost his mother, Aminah, and, soon thereafter, his grandfather, Abdul Mutallib. The care of Muhammad was then taken up by his uncle, Abu Talib. He spent his youth as a shepherd and joined caravans alongside his uncle. He was recognized for his honesty and trustworthiness. Islamic historical accounts say he was also known as Amin (Trustworthy) and Sadeq (Honest). A famous story that illustrates Muhammad's high character is the story of the repair of the Ka'ba. After years of neglect, the structure of the Ka'ba was in disrepair and the Meccans had agreed to rebuild it. When the reconstruction was finished, a dispute arose about which tribe would have the honor of placing the black stone back onto the Ka'ba. The disagreement became heated, and one of those present said that the next person to arrive would be called on to settle the dispute.

Muhammad soon arrived and was informed of the situation. Muhammad counseled for the stone to be placed on a cloak and for members of each tribe to hold an equal part of the cloak. Once raised, the cloak was brought to the Ka'ba. Muhammad put the stone back, but each tribe shared in the act. The sources mention that Muhammad's fair dealing caught the attention of a wealthy businesswoman, an older woman named Khadija. She hired Muhammad to lead a caravan and later asked for his hand in marriage. The trust, honesty, and acumen of Muhammad defines his character for all Muslims.

At the age of 25, Muhammad married Khadija, aged 40. They had six children—two boys and four girls. Both of the boys died in infancy, but the girls survived. Muhammad would often journey outside of the city to spend long periods in reflection, prayer, and meditation—at times for a full month. His chose a cave in Mount Hira to be the focus for his meditation. Islamic tradition holds that inside this cave, Muhammad received the first revelation of the Qur'an and was tasked as the Final Prophet of God. At this time he was 40 years of age.

LIFE OF MUHAMMAD

■ **570 CE:** Muhammad is born in Mecca

■ **576 CE:** He is orphaned with the loss of both parents

■ **595 CE:** Marries Khadija

■ **610 CE:** Receives his first revelation of the Qur'an on Mount Hira

■ **610 CE:** Start of his public preaching

■ **619 CE:** The year of sorrow. Deaths of his wife Khadija and his uncle Abu Talib

■ **620 CE:** *Isra' wal Mi'raj* or The Night Journey

- **622 CE:** The *Hijrah* or migration from Mecca to Madinah—marks the start of the Islamic calendar

- **622 CE:** The Charter of Madinah is drafted, ensuring religious and social freedom for all inhabitants

- **624 CE:** Battle of Badr—a turning point against the Meccan tribes

- **630 CE:** Muhammad and his followers gain control of Mecca without violence—his enemies and the inhabitants of the city are forgiven

- **632 CE:** The Farewell Pilgrimage—the Prophet informs the Muslims that he will soon depart this world

- **632 CE:** Muhammad dies in Madinah

REVELATION OF THE QUR'AN

While in the cave, Muslims believe that a great light surrounded Muhammad. The archangel Gabriel appeared to him and commanded, "Read!"

Muhammad was illiterate and replied that he could not read. The angel repeated the command, and after the third time, Muhammad miraculously began to read the following verses:

> *In the name of God, the all Compassionate, the especially Merciful*
>
> *Read!*
>
> *Read in the name of your Lord who has created—*
>
> *From an embryo created the human*
>
> *Read and your Lord is the most Generous*
>
> *Who taught by the pen*
>
> *Taught the human what he did not know before.*
>
> **(The Qur'an, 96:1–5)**

The overpowering experience compelled Muhammad to return home and tell Khadija and his household what had happened. Muhammad's family memorialized his words, becoming the first believers, the first Muslims. Muslims believe that the sharing of this news and his prophecy marks the beginning of Islam. Muhammad continued to receive the revelation of the Qur'an over a span of 23 years. According to Islamic teachings, the revelation occurred with a varying number of verses over this period; at times there would be no revelation for a number of days or even weeks.

The first occasion of revelation coincides with the Islamic month of Ramadan. As noted earlier, Ramadan is the central period in the year for Muslims to express their devotion and spirituality. The reading of the Qur'an during Ramadan is a ritualized version of the Qur'anic revelation to Muhammad, just as Muhammad's companions and early Muslims would memorize and write down those first revelations. (We will discuss the Qur'an with greater detail in chapter 5.)

FAMILY LIFE

By all Islamic accounts, the marriage of Muhammad and Khadija was harmonious and joyful—except for the loss of their two sons in infancy, a loss that caused tremendous sorrow for the couple. Islamic sources say that Muhammad shed tears at the loss of his children but affirmed his trust in and submission to God. Likewise, Muhammad would fondly remember and praise Khadija long after she died, mentioning that she was pious and truthful and supported him and Islam when Meccans and his own tribe shunned and ostracized him. In addition to their four daughters (Ruqayyah, Zainab, Umm Kulthum, and Fatima), the Prophet's household included his cousin Ali (whom he took under his care) and an adopted son named Zayd. Muhammad married other women after Khadija's death, the two most prominently noted in Islamic tradition being Ayesha and Umm Salama. Muslim sources maintain that the subsequent marriages of the Prophet were entered into to bring affiliation with different tribes, prevent war, and create kinship. None of the other women he married conceived children. Thus, all of

Muhammad's children by blood were through his marriage to Khadija. Islamic tradition says that the Prophet was happy as a husband and father. He also greatly loved and adored his grandchildren, Hassan and Hussein. Narrations mention that he would prolong his prostrations in prayer because the brothers would climb on his back and shoulders while he was praying.

ISLAM'S VIEW ON SATAN

The last chapter of the Qur'an (114) is structured in five verses. It is a meditation and request for security and refuge with God. But from what? The fourth verse tells the answer: "From the evil of the whispering, elusive tempter" (114:4). This is Satan, a figure shared by the other monotheistic faiths, though in differing degrees.

Islam's view on Satan can be summarized with that fourth verse. Satan is a category of "tempters to evil and wickedness," intent on derailing humanity from the realization and worship of God. The Qur'an describes Satan as "an enemy to mankind" (12:5; 35:6; 43:62). He is introduced in the Qur'an as the being who refused God's command in relation to honoring Adam and was cast out by God (2:34).

Islam holds that Satan does not have independent power over humankind, but rather entices, seduces to wrongdoing, and pushes humans to deviate from righteousness and God-consciousness. Because Satan is deceptive and a sworn enemy of humankind, Muslims believe that Satan acts as a necessary challenge for humanity, thereby helping them develop the capacity to withstand temptations and incitements, as well as manifest the great potential humanity possesses. People are responsible for their actions, but the challenge represented by Satan is necessary to develop righteousness and to progress on the spiritual path.

Muslims attest that Satan's misguidance can be averted by adhering to the methods of God-consciousness and piety as explained by Islamic law and teachings. Anyone who succumbs to the temptations of Satan can be redeemed through repentance and increasing righteous acts. "The devil threatens you with poverty and orders you to commit immorality; but God promises you His Forgiveness and bounty. And God is Ample-giving, Knowing" (The Qur'an 2:268).

Early Islam

With the first revealed verses of the Qur'an, Islam began to take root. The first two people to accept the Islamic faith and the prophethood of Muhammad were his wife Khadija and his cousin Ali. There was not an immediate mandate to spread the message to others. This occurred in stages: first to his larger family, then to those in the community who would listen, and finally to all. Muhammad's message centered on a belief in the Oneness of God and equality, two things that were in opposition to wider social practice at the time. The first group of his extended followers were mainly the young, poor, downtrodden, and enslaved.

Muhammad's word spread. It picked up steam among the Meccans. As more people became receptive to the Prophet's message, the ruling elite of Mecca lost patience and felt their power was threatened, fearing a collapse of order. Thus began the period of persecution of Muhammad and his early followers. The persecution ranged from verbal assaults and stone-throwing to the torture and killing of a number of first Muslims. Attempts were made to lure Muhammad with promises of power, wealth, and women, on condition that he cease preaching and agree not to disturb the status quo. Muhammad, however, remained committed to his calling and did not bend.

Muslim historical sources consider this period of Islamic history and revelation as the Meccan period of the prophetic life of Muhammad and Qur'anic revelation. The emphasis during this period was on the spread of belief in and worship of the one true God. Muhammad spent 12 years in Mecca calling people to Islam. He and his family spent two of these years cast out of the city and forced to live in a cave. This was followed by what Muslims call the "Year of Sorrow" for Muhammad, which saw the deaths of his beloved wife Khadija and his uncle Abu Talib.

The death of these two, his main protectors in the web of tribal politics and power brokering, made the situation for the Prophet and his followers bleaker. He sent a group of Muslims as refugees to the Christian kingdom of Abyssinia (now the countries of Eritrea and Ethiopia) to escape persecution in Mecca. However, it was Muhammad's own departure from Mecca that marked the beginning of the Islamic calendar and changed the course of Islam and the world.

KEY CONVERTS

- **Khadija:** The Prophet's first wife and the first woman to accept Islam.

- **Ali:** The Prophet's cousin, raised by him, as well as his son-in-law married to his daughter Fatima. Shi'a Muslims consider him the rightful leader of the Muslim community after Muhammad passed away, and Sunni Muslims regard him as the fourth rightful leader.

- **Abu Talib:** The Prophet's uncle and main guarantor against the Meccan leaders.

- **Abu Bakr al-Siddiq:** A close friend of the Prophet Muhammad and the first caliph. He is also the father of the Prophet's wife Ayesha.

- **'Ammar bin Yasir:** One of the closest companions of the Prophet. According to the Prophet, his death would be at the hands of the unjust.

- **Bilal the Abyssinian:** Formerly enslaved and one of the closest companions of the Prophet. He was freed by Abu Bakr and was asked by the Prophet to hold the role of chanting the call to daily prayers. Additionally, he was appointed minister of the treasury and tasked with distributing funds to the needy.

- **Hamzah:** The uncle of the Prophet. His support of the Prophet is considered pivotal. Known for his bravery and loyalty, he is one of the first martyrs of Islam.

- **Abu Dhar:** Another of the closest companions of the Prophet. His piety and spiritual status are a paragon in Islamic historiography.

- **Omar al-Khattab:** Initially hostile to Islam, he eventually accepted Islam and was a close companion of the Prophet. He was also the second caliph, during a large expansion of Muslim rule.

- **Salman al-Farsi:** Of Persian ethnicity and one of the closest companions of the Prophet. The Prophet is reported to have taken his advice for the Battle of Khandaq.

- **Uthman bin 'Affan:** Another of the close companions of the Prophet. He was the third caliph.

- **Zayd bin Harith:** Raised in the home of the Prophet. He was one of the first Muslims and famous for being the adopted son of the Prophet.

- **Miqdad:** Among the early companions of the Prophet. He was noted for his piety and dedication to the family of the Prophet.

- **Sumayyah:** She is considered the first martyr of Islam and was killed by the Meccans for her refusal to disavow her faith. She is also the mother of 'Ammar bin Yasir.

- **Jabir al-Ansari:** A prominent companion of the Prophet. He narrated a large number of traditions and was noted for his love for the family of the Prophet.

MIGRATION FROM MECCA TO MADINAH

Roughly 280 miles from Mecca was the city of Yathrib, modern-day Madinah (Arabic for "City of the Prophet"). Yathrib was home to diverse people and customs; however, internal disagreements and a power vacuum existed in Yathrib. Word about a new prophet in Arabia was spreading from place to place. A delegation from the city came to Mecca to inquire about and meet the new prophet and ended up inviting him to their city for safety and leadership. Islamic accounts say that Muhammad dispatched a number of his followers ahead to Yathrib. As Muhammad stayed back, the Meccan chieftains were devising a plan to end the challenge of Muhammad and his message. They conspired to strike Muhammad in his sleep and kill him. To prevent retribution against one tribe, it was considered smarter to have a member from each tribe involved in the attack. If this were true, the Quraysh, the Prophet's tribe, could not declare war against all the other tribes to avenge the killing of Muhammad.

Muslim sources relate that the archangel Gabriel informed Muhammad of the plot. Muhammad asked his cousin Ali to sleep in his bed. As the Meccans prepared their attack, Muhammad and Abu Bakr, one of his close friends and one of the earliest individuals to accept Islam, slipped out of Mecca for Yathrib. The Meccans soon discovered that Ali was sleeping in the Prophet's bed and followed in hot pursuit. Muhammad and Abu Bakr sought refuge in a cave. The Meccans came near the cave, but did not discover them. The Qur'an mentions that Muhammad remained confident that God would protect them and said to Abu Bakr, "Don't grieve" (The Qur'an: 9:40).

The Hijrah or migration to Yathrib marks a turning point in Islamic history for a number of reasons. It is the start of the Islamic calendar—the Hijri calendar—corresponding to the year 622 CE of the Gregorian calendar. In Yathrib, the Prophet established the first mosque and saw his role extend to contexts such as judge, mediator, ruler of a diverse people, and military commander. Muhammad's focus was on the maintenance of a harmonious society in Yathrib and the maturing of the Muslims' understanding of Islam.

This period is highlighted by the signing of a charter or constitution known as the Charter of Madinah, as the city was now renamed to honor the Prophet. The document established Madinah as a plural and multireligious society, ruled by justice and fairness. The charter committed to ending war and conflicts between the different tribes, including Jews and other groups. The Prophet was winning over new converts and was intent on establishing a society highlighted by justice and compassion, not tribal affinity or class.

KEY BATTLES

Unlike during his period in Mecca, the Prophet Muhammad was now the leader of a society and a bigger target for the Meccans and their allied tribes. The Meccan period was one in which Muslims were not allowed to defend themselves. But in Madinah, new revelations enlightened the Prophet, informing him that Muslims can fight those who fight them. Although the verses related to fighting allowed Muslims the right to defend themselves and Madinah against outside forces, there were strict rules and requirements regarding combat and ensuring that these battles were defensive battles. The Qur'an is emphatic on this point: Here are the key battles of the subsequent period:

> *Fight in God's cause against those who fight you, but do not transgress. Surely, God does not like the transgressors.* **(The Qur'an, Chapter 2, Verse 190)**

Here are the key battles of the subsequent period:

THE BATTLE OF BADR: Muslims, though outnumbered three to one, defeated the Meccans. Muslims considered this a miracle from God and a sign of validity for Islam.

THE BATTLE OF BANU QAYNUQA: A Muslim victory, after which they displayed their mercy and did not harm prisoners. This was a common Muslim practice.

THE BATTLE OF UHUD: Muslims were defeated after a number of fighters broke rank to collect the spoils of war rather than press the attack. As a result, the Muslim positions were overtaken. Muhammad was injured in battle.

THE BATTLE OF KHANDAQ: Madinah was surrounded by the Meccans and their allied tribes. The Muslims dug a moat around the city as a defensive strategy. The Muslim victory in this battle was a major turning point and led to a number of tribes converting to Islam.

THE BATTLE OF KHAIBAR: A key battle that established the Muslims as tough and keenly strategic fighters.

THE VICTORY OF MECCA: The Prophet and his army marched on Mecca after the Meccans broke a peace treaty. The Meccans surrendered without a fight and the Prophet Muhammad offered his customary mercy and forgiveness and did not attack and plunder the town. He is reported to have said: "I shall speak to you as [Prophet] Joseph spoke to his brothers: 'There is no reproach against you today; God will forgive. He is the most Merciful and the most Compassionate'" (The Qur'an 12:92). The Ka'ba was emptied of idols and proclaimed as the site of worship of the one true God.

FINAL YEARS

In 632 CE, Muhammad performed his final pilgrimage. On the journey back to Madinah, Muhammad commanded the Muslims to stop at a pond called Ghadir Khumm. There, he informed the community that he would not live for much longer and announced that his cousin and son-in-law, Ali, would be the leader of the Muslims after Muhammad's death. In his last days, Muhammad was bedridden, surrounded by his family, and visited by companions. Muhammad passed away in the year 632 CE. Muslims grieved and mourned the news of his passing, but soon, visible and impactful disagreements surfaced. In the next chapter on the Shi'a and Sunni branches of Islam, we will explore the fallout from the death of Muhammad and the struggle for succession.

CHAPTER 4

The Shi'a-Sunni Split

With the death of the Prophet, the Muslim community split. The schism was related to the issue of leadership after Muhammad's death. Muslims agreed that prophethood ended with Muhammad; however, there was great disagreement about what to do next. A leader was needed, but who that person was to be became the heart of the struggle between Shi'a and Sunni Muslims.

Shi'as believe that the Prophet Muhammad, following God's command, announced to the community that Ali was to be the leader (*mawla*), of the community after him. They hold that this leadership (*Imamate*) includes both political and spiritual authority. Moreover, they hold that the lineage of leadership continued in the family of Muhammad. Sunnis, on the other hand, maintain that the Prophet did not necessarily mandate Ali as his successor, leaving the issue for the people to decide. They contest that mawla means "friend," differing from the Shi'a interpretation. They maintain that the community selected a number of individuals as the caliphs or rulers.

These Shi'a-Sunni differences of opinion within the Muslim community endure today. It is important to note that the Shi'a-Sunni matter is not similar to that of Catholics and Protestants. The Shi'a-Sunni disagreement appeared immediately after Muhammad's death and did not come centuries after the establishment of Islam, as was the case for Christianity during the Reformation. Shi'as and Sunnis believe in the same Qur'an. When it comes to Islamic law, Shi'as and Sunnis are in agreement on a majority of issues, but the central issue of leadership remains. Historically, different governments and movements have attempted to exploit the differences between the two communities and charge the other as non-Muslim. Sunni extremist groups routinely target Shi'a Muslims. Each respective group has made attempts at combating propaganda and misinformation about themselves with a greater call toward unity and rereading of Islamic history.

This chapter will discuss the two main schools of thought in Islam: Shi'a and Sunni. We will review their historical trajectory and their impact on Muslim relations today.

Leadership after Muhammad

As the message of Islam spread, the future of the community and the role of leadership were important considerations. The unfolding of events and conflicting claim to leadership after Prophet Muhammad caused major disagreements among Muslims. These disagreements remain today. We look now at the events after the Prophet's death and discuss the major areas of contention about leadership of the community.

THE CALIPHS

The passing of Muhammad occurred after a number of contesting groups developed that were intent on asserting their right to leadership. This included the people of Madinah, migrants from Mecca, and the family of the Prophet. An unsystematic gathering by some Madinans and a few Meccans eventually chose Muhammad's friend and father-in-law, Abu Bakr, as the caliph—Arabic for "leader"—of the community. The Prophet's family, clan, and a number of prominent companions rejected this assertion and maintained that the Prophet had named Ali as the rightful leader of the Muslim community. This area of Islamic history is very charged and sensitive for Muslims (for a deeper study of the history of this disagreement, see Recommended Reading and Resources on page 160.)

Abu Bakr was now in old age. He had been among the first individuals to embrace Islam and also had migrated with Muhammad to Madinah. He was the father of the Prophet's wife Ayesha.

Abu Bakr only ruled for two years, and upon his death, he chose Omar al-Khattab to be the next caliph of the Muslims.

Omar al-Khattab, initially resolute in his animosity toward Islam, eventually embraced Islam and joined the ranks of the Prophet's companions. His conversion to Islam is a source of inspiration for many Muslims. Many Muslims also remember him for his role in expanding Muslim rule to other lands. He ruled for 10 years but was assassinated by a servant. Before Omar's assassination, he selected a group of six individuals to choose the next caliph.

Uthman bin 'Affan was chosen by this group as the third caliph. His rule was the longest of the first four caliphs—commonly referred to as the *Rashidun* or rightly guided. Uthman's rule was marked by a liberality in spending from the Muslim treasury and favoritism toward his tribe. This resulted in growing criticism and unrest that eventually led to his assassination.

At this point the community turned to Ali and selected him as the caliph. In addition to his intimate bond with the Prophet, he was revered as a fearless warrior and seen as the reason Muslims gained victory in many of their battles. Ali's personality and rule were marked by an emphasis on justice, the Qur'an, and mysticism. This led to a number of challenges stemming from the tribe of Uthman. Ali's rule saw a number of contentious challenges and battles. He ruled for five years and was assassinated while in prostration during prayer.

The assassination of Ali resulted in a number of factions and changes in leadership. Power and rule shifted away from an attempt to adhere to Islam and the example of the Prophet and toward what can be described as a type of kingship or authoritarianism. Sunni Muslims consider the rule of the first four Rashidun Caliphs to be a period of proper and pious governance. Let us now consider the view of the Shi'a.

FOLLOWERS OF ALI

Ali was raised by the Prophet and, alongside Khadija, was the first to accept Islam. He was the son of the Prophet's uncle, Abu Talib, who took care of Muhammad after his grandfather passed away. In addition to being Muhammad's cousin, Ali also married Muhammad's beloved daughter Fatima. Muslim sources are in agreement that Ali possessed the qualities of a revered and fearless warrior and was a representation of the epitome of upright conduct and bravery in Islam. Muslims unanimously accept that Ali was of uniquely special spiritual and intellectual intelligence. Muhammad stated: "I am the city of knowledge and Ali is its gate" (Hadith 3723).

Ali's special relationship to the Prophet seems to not have been merely that of blood but of an esoteric spiritual component, too. Recognizing this, a group from among the companions of Muhammad proclaimed themselves the Shi'a of Ali. The term *shi'a* means partisan, supporter, or follower. In this case, it refers specifically to those individuals who held that Ali was the true successor of the Prophet Muhammad in the leadership of the Muslim community. They maintained that this was not simply their preference but what the Prophet (and by extension God) wanted. The Shi'a still consider the rule of the first three caliphs to be an infringement of Ali's authority and against the wishes of Muhammad.

Certain Muslims and allied Arab tribes were uneasy about leadership continuing in the family of the Prophet Muhammad. Many also held animosity toward Ali for killing their relatives in battle, or they just considered him too young. Nonetheless, Ali and his supporters maintained his claim and emphasized statements of Muhammad for support of it. However, Ali prioritized the cohesion of the Muslim community and counseled the other caliphs. Ali's merits are uniformly accepted by Muslims. His letters, sermons, and sayings are commonly referenced and collected under the title *Nahj al-Balagha: The Peak of Eloquence*. Among the collection is a letter to his governor in Egypt. The letter lays out Ali's vision of how an Islamic government and rule should be. Ali reminds the governor that "People are of two kinds: either your equal in faith, or your equal in humanity" (*Nahj al-Balagha*, Letter 53).

SUFISM: THE MYSTICAL ORDER

Sufism, or *Tasawwuf*, is the inner, mystical teachings of Islam. It is not a separate school of thought, such as the Shi'a and Sunni, but an orientation toward a more subtle experience and understanding of Islam. The term derives from the word meaning "pure" or "wool." Sufism emphasizes the purification of the heart, asceticism, and the inner realities of Islamic teachings. Using verses of the Qur'an and sayings of the Prophet, Sufi philosophy maintains that the heart must be purified in order for it to awaken to the reality of existence and God. A purified heart will ensure that the ego is overpowered and reality is witnessed. Sufis have a three-pronged approach for this: *Shari'a* (Islamic law), *tariqa* (Sufi order or path), and *haqiqa* (truth or reality).

Following demanding regimens of prayers, contemplation, *dhikr* (to lovingly recall and utter the names of God and devotional prayers), fasting, and other actions, the traveler (Sufi) progresses on the path of the heart's purification. The path is formed by states and stations. States can be brief experiences of insight and spiritual ecstasy, but stations are more lasting experiences of spiritual progress.

The binary states of Sufi and non-Sufi did not historically exist in ways we find today. Eventually, certain Sufi orders were formed either by teachers or by their students and followers. Sufis trace their paths back to the Prophet via Ali. There are numerous Sufi orders in America. Concurrently, a number of individuals and groups appropriate Sufism but contradict traditional Sufi teachings and literature. Erasing Islam from Sufism by some in the West is problematic and connected to a precarious history.

Sufis are historically profound contributors to Islamic art, literature, and music. Of particular importance is the poetry of individuals such as Hallaj, Ibn 'Arabi, Ibn al-Farid, Sana'i, Mawlana of Balkh (Rumi), Hafez, Yunus Emre, and others. Sufism emphasizes the importance of love in the worship and realization of God. Sufi shrines, which hold the bodies of Sufi masters and saints, are frequent sites of visitation and prayers throughout the Muslim world. The Sufis are often subjected to violence and attacks by extremist groups.

Shi'a and Sunni Schools of Thought

As previously established, the most prominent difference, both past and present, between the Shi'a and Sunni schools of thought is the issue of leadership and succession after the Prophet Muhammad. This issue remains at the heart of the divergence and impacts other areas of interpretation.

Shi'as believe that leadership in the spiritual and political realms for the community is maintained with the *Ahlul Bayt*, or People of the House. The term refers specifically to the Prophet Muhammad, Ali, Fatima, and their sons, Hassan and Hussein. This continuation in leadership and authority after Muhammad's death begins with Ali, then Hassan, then Hussein, and thereafter with specific individuals from his progeny. Within the Shi'a there are a number of different groups. The most prominent are the Twelver Shi'as, who believe that the total number of leaders from the Ahlul Bayt is twelve.

Sunnis also revere the family of the Prophet and consider them paragons of piety and goodness. However, they maintain that the companions of the Prophet hold the right to leadership and selection. For Shi'as, the companions of the Prophet Muhammad are not of equal standing. Shi'as categorize the companions as being of various levels of spiritual attainment and conviction and maintain that some companions deviated from Islamic teachings.

In matters of worship, dietary laws, acts, and general belief, the Shi'a and Sunni are commonly in agreement with only a few minor differences. Both schools agree on the five required daily prayers and the number of units for each prayer. However, all Shi'as pray with their hands open, while some Sunnis pray with their hands crossed on their stomach and others pray with their hands open. For dietary considerations, Sunnis consider anything of the sea to be permissible for consumption. Shi'as, alternatively, accept only certain types of seafood to be valid for consumption. In deriving Islamic law, Shi'as consider *aql* (reason) as the fourth source of law, while for Sunnis it is achieved via *qiyas* (analogy).

In the narrations and reports of the life of the Prophet Muhammad, Sunnis mainly rely on the transmission of narrations from the Prophet's companions. However, Shi'as refer to what has been transmitted by the Prophet's family. They also consider the sayings of the Ahlul Bayt to hold spiritual authority.

Although their disagreements have led to divergent interpretations of certain aspects of Islamic practice and belief, Shi'as and Sunnis still agree on issues such as the veracity of the Qur'an, angels, prophethood, the Day of Judgment, and so forth.

MODERN-DAY DIFFERENCES

There are a number of countries in the Muslim world with Shi'a-majority populations such as Azerbaijan, Bahrain, Lebanon, Iraq, and Iran. A number of other countries have sizeable Shi'a-minority populations of 21 to 30 percent, including Afghanistan, Yemen, Pakistan, Turkey, Saudi Arabia, Syria, and Kuwait.

Shi'as view the Ahlul Bayt as divine leaders committed to justice and righteousness. Moreover, they commemorate the martyrdom of individuals from the Ahlul Bayt, especially the grandson of the Prophet, Hussein—who, alongside a number of other members of the Prophet's family and his companions, was martyred in Karbala, in what is now Iraq. Shi'as consider this a watershed moment in Islamic history. Hussein stood for the purity of Islam, which they argue is rooted in justice, human dignity, righteousness, and sincere worship of God. The ruler that killed him, Yazid, represented the deviations that occurred as a result of the Muslim community turning away from the Ahlul Bayt. To this day, Shi'as and Sunnis maintain that Yazid was unjust and spiritually corrupt.

The annual commemoration of this event in the month of Muharram (the first month of the Islamic calendar) is considered a sociopolitical-spiritual awakening and movement for Shi'as. It is a somber time, and intricate ceremonies—which include recitation of the Qur'an, passionate speeches, poetry lamenting the martyrdom of Hussein, and mourning—are conducted by Shi'as worldwide. The commemoration reaches a climax on the tenth of the month, Ashura—the day that Hussein was brutally martyred and the Prophet's family chained and paraded through town. Sunni Muslims also revere Hussein but do not generally discuss the matter widely. For many Sunnis, Ashura's significance is tied to a special fast that results in sins being forgiven. Shi'as do not accept this as valid and often criticize Sunnis for not prioritizing the martyrdom of Hussein. There are Sunni Muslims who either participate in the wider mourning ceremonies with Shi'a Muslims or hold their own commemorations for the Martyrs of Karbala.

Shrines of saints and righteous believers are common throughout the Muslim world. Some fringe elements in Islam claim that visiting shrines is deviant, signifying the worship of something other than God. The counterpoint offered by both traditional Sunni and Shi'a Muslims is that the worship is not directed to the individual buried, but that the recitation of the Qur'an, prayers, and supplication are rather addressed to God. The space of the shrine serves as the conduit for God's special mercy and favor. Shi'as consider the Ahlul Bayt to be infallible. Their role is the elucidation of the Qur'an and the preservation of the teachings and way of the Prophet. The disagreements between Muslims are often politicized and weaponized. The history and nuances of the differences of opinion between Muslims is complex and has an impact to this day.

CHAPTER 5

Significance of the Qur'an

For Muslims, the Qur'an is the direct revelation of God to the Prophet Muhammad. In other words, the Qur'an is the verbatim revelation from God without any change, addition, or alteration by the Prophet. Muslims consider the Qur'an as God's final revelation to humanity and hold that the Qur'an has not changed, nor will it be altered. The Qur'an plays an active role in the lives of Muslims and is experienced both orally and aurally. The Qur'an is both revelation and relation, sight and sound, reading and receiving. Because it is considered the direct and unchangeable word of God, all other aspects of religion and sources must be in agreement with the Qur'an—this includes the numerous sayings and statements attributed to the Prophet Muhammad. With that in mind, it can be said that the Qur'an is the supreme source of Islam.

In addition to being read, memorized, written as art and calligraphy, listened to, and venerated by Muslims, the Qur'an has a number of scholarly sciences associated with it. These include the science of interpretation, mystical meanings, recitation, history, and many others. For Muslims, the Qur'an is a miraculous text both in content and in its role in the spiritual cosmology of existence. The Qur'an is a manifestation of God's mercy and the reading and recitation of the text are counted as participation in and reception of that mercy.

How the Qur'an Was Revealed

The Qur'an is a collection of chapters—114 in total—composed of verses. The chapters are called *surahs* in Arabic and the verses are called *ayahs*. It is important to clarify the unique nature of a chapter of the Qur'an. A chapter can range from three verses to 286 verses—the longest chapter in the Qur'an. This of course doesn't align with our general understanding of a book chapter. Additionally, the chapters of the Qur'an are not arranged chronologically in the order in which they were revealed. In other words, the first chapter of the Qur'an does not include the very first verses that were revealed to the Prophet Muhammad. It was previously discussed that the first were verses revealed to the Prophet Muhammad while he was in spiritual seclusion in a cave on Mount Hira. Those initial verses, rather than appearing as chapter 1, are part of chapter 96 of the Qur'an.

This tells us that a chapter of the Qur'an can be composed of verses that were revealed to the Prophet at different times through the agency of the archangel Gabriel. The entire span of the Qur'anic revelation is considered to be 20 years. Moreover, Qur'anic chapters are categorized as either Meccan or Madinan, which refers to whether the verses were revealed to the Prophet in Mecca or after his migration to Madinah. There are 86 Meccan and 28 Madinan chapters. The Meccan chapters tend to be shorter and deal with the general principles of faith: belief in the Oneness of God, the Day of Judgment, doing good, etc. The Madinan chapters are more attuned to the specifics of the faith: fasting, prayer, charity, issues dealing with law, and similar matters. They deal with the expanded practice and reality of the Muslims as believers.

The verses of the Qur'an carry the meaning of signs. For Muslims, each verse of the Qur'an is in actuality a sign from and of God. The Qur'an is in Arabic, and every Muslim learns to memorize chapters and verses from the Qur'an in Arabic—whether they are a native Arabic speaker or not. American converts to Islam, for example, will eventually memorize chapters of the Qur'an and conduct their prayers in Arabic. To help with facilitating the understanding of the Qur'an in Arabic, translations are directly referenced to the meaning of the verses to help non-Arabic speakers learn as close as possible the original intent of the text.

Islam considers the Qur'an to be a work of unique and miraculous eloquence that carries a spiritual power and energy that cannot be replicated. For Muslims, the spoken language of the Qur'an is considered of special miraculous eloquence. The Qur'an arose in a preliterate society that relied on memorization and recitation. To this day, the processes of revelation, dissemination of the verses by the Prophet, and memorization of the revealed text and the written corpus of the Qur'an are all thought to be divinely sanctioned and protected. As a result, the Qur'an is understood to be not only a work of history but also a present text that carries an active, sacred presence. As such it must be engaged with, experienced, and understood. Muslims feel that the full reality of Qur'anic teachings can only be realized with great acumen and spiritual purification.

Importance of the Qur'an

The Qur'an is uniquely interwoven in Muslim spiritual practice and philosophy. As the verbatim revelation of God, Muslims recite, listen to, memorize, explain, and artistically express the Arabic verses and seek out their inner content and truth. Muslims know a number of chapters of the Qur'an by heart, and they recite these verses in Arabic during their daily prayers. The Qur'an is considered the ultimate, unchanged source of truth in Islam, and everything—from sayings attributed to the Prophet to theological and mystical views—needs to be in harmony with it. Thus it is important for us to explore some aspects of the Qur'anic message.

MAJOR THEMES

The Qur'an has a number of overarching themes, though it is neither chronologically nor thematically organized. One surah can deal with a number of themes. Additionally, the verses and themes of the Qur'an are better understood when read collectively. The verses should be read in the context of their respective chapters as well as their larger thematic realities. One cannot engage with all or most of the themes of the Qur'an. This section will broach a few major themes.

MERCY: This is the most significant theme of the Qur'an. Consider the very first verse in the Qur'an, "In the name of God, the Compassionate (Ar-Rahman), the uniquely Merciful (Ar-Rahim)" (1:1). This formulaic verse is also recited before all but one chapter of the Qur'an. Numerous other verses maintain this central theme throughout the Qur'an, including "And my Mercy encompasses all things" (The Qur'an 7:156), and "And your God is the One God: there is no deity but Him, the Most Merciful, the Compassionate" (The Qur'an 2:163).

JUSTICE: The Qur'an is deeply focused on justice. The issue of justice has a twofold component. First, God is just: "Truly God does not do injustice by as much as an atom's weight; and if there be a good deed, He will multiply it and bestow out of His grace a mighty reward " (The Qur'an 4:40). Though all power is God's alone, God is not unjust even to those who disbelieve (The Qur'an 36:54).

Justice is expected from and commanded of humans. "Surely, God commands you [people] to return things entrusted to you to their rightful owners, and, if you judge between people, to do so with justice: God's instructions to you are excellent, for He hears and see everything" (The Qur'an 4:58). Another verse states, "God commands justice, beautiful acts, and generosity toward relatives and He forbids what is shameful, blameworthy, and oppressive. He instructs you, so that you may take heed" (The Qur'an 16:90).

PROPHETHOOD: The Qur'an heavily emphasizes both the divine institution of prophethood and aspects of the lives of prophets. These examples come together to form a collective understanding of both the challenges and successes of prophethood. Many verses of the Qur'an ask the reader to recall and think about certain episodes from the lives of prophets sacred to Islam.

REFLECTION: The Qur'an holds that textual and meditative reflection is key to the realization of truth and reality. "Do they not reflect on the Qur'an? Or are their hearts locked up?" (The Qur'an 47:24). The Qur'an qualifies discerning and understanding people as those who "think deeply about the creation of the heavens and the earth, (saying): 'Our Lord! You have not created (all) this without purpose, glory to You! Give us salvation from the torment of the Fire" (The Qur'an 3:191). Another verse connects contemplation and travel: "Have they, then, never journeyed about the earth, letting their hearts gain wisdom, and causing their ears to hear? It is not people's eyes that are blind, but their hearts within their chests" (The Qur'an 22:46).

FORGIVENESS AND HOPE: Forgiveness is a major theme of the Qur'anic ethos. "Say, [God says], My servants who have harmed yourselves by your own excess (in evil deeds and sin), do not despair of God's mercy. God forgives all sins: He is truly the Most Forgiving, the Most Merciful. Turn to your Lord. Submit to Him before the punishment overtakes you and you can be no longer helped" (The Qur'an 39:53–54). This theme can be combined with another prominent theme: hope. "The Forgiver of faults and the Acceptor of repentance." (The Qur'an 40:3; see also 39:9).

EQUITY: This key theme relates to socioeconomic matters in general, but it is also linked to justice; though closely related, the Qur'an uses different terms. "Believers! Maintain equity and bear witness to God (in truth and justice), even it if is against yourselves, your parents, or your close relatives. Whether the person is rich or poor. . . . [r]efrain from following your own desire, so that you can act justly—if you distort or neglect equity, God is fully aware of what you do" (The Qur'an 4:135). In another verse, the Prophet Muhammad is commanded, "Say, my Lord has commanded equity" (The Qur'an 7:29).

NATURE: For the Qur'an, nature is a sign of God, active in the worship of God, and one of the spaces for spiritual discovery for Muslims. From the Qur'anic perspective, each aspect of nature and phenomena, when reflected upon and witnessed, points not just to itself but to God. Humanity is called not just to reflect on nature but to experience and harmonize with it. "And the (unique) servants of the Merciful Lord are they who walk on the earth in humbleness, and when the ignorant address them, they say: Peace" (The Qur'an 25:63). Another such verse is

> *Control of the heavens and earth belongs to Him. Everything is brought back to God. He makes night merge into day and day into night. He knows what is in every heart.* **(The Qur'an 57:5- 6)**

HUMANITY: A large number of verses deal with humanity. "O humankind, We have created you all from a single man and single woman, and made you into races and tribes so that you should get to know one another. The most honorable of you with God is the most God-conscious. God is Knowing, Aware" (The Qur'an 49:13).

Other major themes of the Qur'an include the remembrance of God, the hereafter, charity, patience, revelation, love and respect for parents, and death.

SURAH AL-FATIHA
"THE OPENING"

Sura Al-Fatiha ("The Opening") is the first chapter of the Qur'an. Its verses are a prayer for God's guidance and stress the Lordship and Mercy of God. This chapter has a special role in daily prayers, being recited at the start of each unit of prayer.

In the name of God, bismillah
the Unconditionally Loving, ar-Rahmaan
the Mercifully Loving, ar-Raheem
grateful praise is due God, alhamdulillaah
the Lord-Sustainer of all worlds, rabb il-'alameen
the Unconditionally loving, ar-Rahmaan
the Mercifully Loving, ar-Raheem
Ruler of the Day of Judgment, Maaliki yawm ad-deen!
Only You do we devotedly worship, iyyaka na'budu
and from only You do we seek assistance,
wa-iyyaka nasta'een.
Guide us on the straight path, ihdina
s-siraat al-mustaqeem
the path of those, siraat alladheena
upon whom You have bestowed bounty,
an'amta 'alayhim
not of those who've received anger, ghayr il-maghdubi
'alayhim and not of those who stray, wa-la d-daalleen

*Translation primarily done by Dr. Alan Godlas

SIGNIFICANT VERSES

The most commonly recited verses of the Qur'an are the seven verses that form the opening chapter. Three verses of chapter 112 are also recited daily. These tend to be the first verses that Muslims learn and are an integral part of the daily prayers. Other shorter chapters, such as 97, 103, 108, 113, and 114, are widely known and recited. The following is a brief review of some significant verses.

Muslims feel that certain verses possess unique qualities, such as blessings, mercy, and safeguards against calamity and harm. It is common to find verses written in calligraphy or used in other cultural contexts in Muslim homes.

The following passage of the Qur'an is also frequently cited by Muslims: "So truly where there is hardship there is also ease; truly with hardship there is also ease" (The Qur'an 94:5–6).

Other widely known verses also contain supplications, or humble requests: "Our Lord, give us good in this world and in the Hereafter, and protect us from the torment of the Fire" (The Qur'an 2:201) and "My Lord, increase me in knowledge" (The Qur'an 20:114). And there are verses that remind adherents about patience and grace, especially during adversity: "Surely, God is with those who are gracefully patient" (The Qur'an 8:46). Another verse recited often is "Indeed God and His Angels send blessings and serenity on the Prophet. O you who believe, pray for benediction on him, and give him greetings of peace" (The Qur'an 33:56).

Lastly, among the key verses in the Qur'an is: "Surely, we are God's and to God is our return" (The Qur'an 2:156).

Interpretation of the Qur'an

The Qur'an includes verses that are "clear" as well as those that are "allegorical" (The Qur'an 3:7). Muslims have understood that the Qur'an has multiple layers of meaning in its verses. The interpretation of the Qur'an is a science of scholarship and an enduring part of Islamic history and spirituality. We turn now to the interpretation of this holy book.

WHY ARABIC?

"We have sent it down as an Arabic Qur'an so that you might encompass it with your reason" (The Qur'an 12:2). This and other similar verses emphasize the Qur'an's revelation in Arabic. Muslims maintain that since God chose the Arabic language for the final revelation to humankind, the original Arabic text possesses the ultimate revelation, spiritual power, and majesty. Every Muslim knows at least one chapter of the Qur'an in the original Arabic. This connects Muslims back to the Prophet Muhammad himself and, as they see it, the true word of God. Islam considers the Qur'an transcendent and miraculous. Muslims believe that the Qur'an has not been changed and will never be changed or altered.

For Muslims, reading, memorizing, and listening to the Qur'an in Arabic establishes a direct link with the Divine and the sacred presence of revelation. Further, by reading and memorizing the Qur'an, Muslims are participating in the preservation of the text in its original form. Muslims believe that the language of revelation carries multiple layers of meaning and nuance that are not found in the same way in other languages.

Reading the Qur'an is considered to be tremendously rewarding—not just in the context of understanding and guidance but also, quite literally, because such active engagement with the Qur'an leads to reward and forgiveness. Islamic tradition mentions that every letter of the Qur'an recited counts as 10 blessings and also leads to the forgiveness of 10 sins. The Qur'an is viewed as a manifestation of God and a direct extension of spiritual sacredness; it is accessible to all people and not confined to those whose mother tongue is Arabic, despite the fact that Arabic is held to be so uniquely sacred in Islam. The Qur'an is a very eloquent and poetic text, though it is not a book of poetry. There is still poetic harmony in the verses, and listening to them is a moving activity for Muslims.

DIFFERENCES IN INTERPRETATION

The interpretation of and attempt to understand the meaning, context, and nuances of Qur'anic verses are major aspects of Islamic scholarship. Given the status the Qur'an holds, interpretation is a very systematic science of scholarship in Islam. The engagement with this science requires training and qualifications in a number of fields, including philology, Arabic grammar and morphology, rhetoric, jurisprudence, causes of revelation (reviewing the context in which verses were revealed and whether the verse has a specific or general application), the science of recitations, and other matters. The body of commentary and explication aimed at explaining the Qur'an is known as *tafsir* in Arabic.

Individuals without scholarly training cannot appropriately engage in tafsir. Naturally, different approaches and points of focus exist in tafsir works. Some works focus on the rhetoric and linguistics of the Qur'an, for example. Tafsirs that center on citing prophetic narrations—hadith—related to different verses of the Qur'an or its topics are another example. By utilizing the hadith (which are not part of the Qur'an), these interpretations attempt to arrive at the correct meaning of Qur'anic verses. Some approaches tend to be theological in nature. There are also a vast number of mystical tafsirs. Such interpretations strive to explain the deeper meanings and subtleties of revelation in order to highlight the mystical intensity of Qur'anic verses. Lastly, a number of interpretations are organized thematically (not just in the order of the Qur'an's index) and have wide reception among scholars and the general public.

Approaches to tafsir can range from the very literal to the mystical and nuanced, or a combination of these. Highly regarded works of interpretation are translated into the many different languages Muslims speak—including English. Interpretation of Qur'anic verses and commentary on them is a frequent component of lectures at mosques and Islamic centers, as well as on Islamic television and on the Internet.

DAILY USE

Given the centrality of the Qur'an in the life of committed Muslims, daily use of the text is an integral component of Muslim life. There are expected protocols when holding or touching the text of the Qur'an. Islamic law maintains that ritual ablution (discussed in chapter 2) is required before Muslims may touch the text of the Qur'an. Moreover, the Qur'an is generally wrapped in a scarf or other fabric and placed on the highest shelf. When first holding the Qur'an, Muslims do so with two hands and kiss the book as a sign of care and recognition of its sacredness.

The Qur'an generated a salient shift toward literacy and language in Arabia and the wider Muslim world. One of the results of this new literary orientation was Arabic calligraphy. Calligraphy and spiritual aesthetics form a key portion of Islamic material culture. Muslim homes often have verses of the Qur'an in different calligraphic or material forms displayed on their walls.

Alongside the daily recitation of Qur'anic verses and the five prayers, Muslims mention verses from the Qur'an when leaving the house or in prayerful supplication. The first verse of the Qur'an, "In the name of God, the Compassion, the uniquely Merciful," is recited invarious aspects of daily life such as getting up, starting an activity, or eating food.

Muslims learn to read and memorize the Qur'an from a young age. There are schools that specialize in the instruction of Qur'anic memorization, but such instruction can also occur under the guidance of a local scholar or family member. In the United States, mosques generally have Sunday school where children and youth learn to read the Qur'an and memorize from it. There are options for older students as well.

The Qur'an is an integral part of Muslim life on occasions both of joy and sorrow. For example, Muslim funeral services include recitations of the Qur'an and an entire reading of the Qur'an is completed by the family and community on behalf of the soul of the departed. This is done by participants volunteering to read various parts of the Qur'an and thus completing a collective reading.

Muslims believe that listening to the Qur'an places the individual in God's mercy and is spiritually purifying. Individual Muslims specialize as reciters by studying the art of *tajwid* (Arabic for "beautification"). This art focuses on the proper pronunciation and rules of reading the Qur'an, as well as vocal training. The Qur'an should be recited in a methodic and melodic voice. Each person's voice varies but each voice can be beautified when melodically carrying the Qur'an.

CHAPTER 6

Islamic Laws

One of the hallmarks of Islam is an official system of law, a normative system of what is considered proper and improper behavior. Earlier, we discussed that Islam believes in the notion of free will. How does free will coexist with law? The answer, according to Islam, is that humans are free to choose, but given the differences of personal preference and opinion there needs to be a standard system that identifies what the correct choice is, and then humans are free to choose or ignore it. Muslims consider law to be one of the most prominent aspects of a religious life and orientation. Moreover, laws maintain harmony in society and establish guidelines that protect the spiritual as well as the physical well-being of the individual. Islamic law is comprehensive—it impacts all aspects of the lived and daily experiences of Muslims. This can touch on matters of belief, dietary laws, medical ethics, business, marriage, and numerous other things. For Muslims, irrespective of their religious leanings, law impacts their lives, shapes and informs their identity, and connects them to religious practice.

Since humans are free to choose, the extent of adherence to Islamic laws varies from place to place and person to person. Additionally, there are instances wherein local culture is presented as Islamic law. This chapter will introduce Islamic law as well as the content and fields from which Islamic laws are derived.

SUNNAH AND HADITH

The Prophet Muhammad plays a particularly essential role in Islam—not only since he is considered the Final Prophet, but because he is the best example of how to lead one's life. In relation to the role and example of the Prophet Muhammad, Muslims rely on the reports and narrative of his life. In studying and learning the life of the Prophet, Muslims look for clear instances of his acts and imitate these acts or their spirit in their day-to-day lives. The Prophet is considered the most complete or perfect being (*al-Insan al-Kamil*). In order for Muslims to grow in their awareness and perfection (both worldly and spiritual), they should follow the Prophet's example.

The detailed examples of how and when Muhammad did certain things is gathered as *Sunnah*. The Arabic term has many different meanings, but it can best be understood as the "art of action." In addition to the category of actions and ways in which the Prophet lived, there is also the category of his sayings, the hadith. These two categories, in addition to the Qur'an, form the most important sources for Islamic law and religious life for Muslims. Islam is concentrated on spirituality as practice, a complete way of life, and is oriented toward a harmonious existence. This harmony is understood to only occur with God-consciousness, awareness of the Divine, and witnessing the signs (*ayat*). The presence and clarification of laws are vital for Muslims in achieving sacred harmony.

WHAT ARE SUNNAH?

The Sunnah are the art of prophetic action. They highlight the lived experience of the Prophet and chronicle his daily existence. Since the Prophet is considered to be a perfect human and is introduced in the Qur'an as someone who possesses exalted character, Islamic spirituality looks to the Prophet as the source and model of how to live. The Prophet Muhammad, though perfect, was not divine. He lived among the people as a man, albeit a perfect one. Islamic teachings maintain that humans need human prophets—individuals who can be relatable but also exemplary and infallible.

Muhammad is the ideal that Muslims should aspire to be. They mold their actions and character in accordance to his life via the Sunnah, which cover a very wide breadth. The Prophet is considered to be the "speaking Qur'an." In other words, the Sunnah are seen as the explanation and manifestation of Qur'anic verses through Muhammad. The Qur'an maintains the essential need for the daily prayers, and Muslims understand how to perform those prayers by the examples of Muhammad in the Sunnah. According to the Sunnah, the Prophet is reported to have always had a smile on his face and greeted people as he passed by them. The Sunnah include teachings on clothing, hygiene, and certain supplementary prayers and spiritual practices; they record how the Prophet sat, what he wore, that he would stand when his daughter Fatima would enter (to show love and respect to her), how he would help with housework and care for the needy, and many other realms of activity.

HOW ARE THE SUNNAH INTERPRETED?

Unlike the Qur'an, which Muslims consider to be unchanged and miraculous, as well as existing in its current verses during the time of the Muhammad, Muslims do not consider everything that is reported in Sunnah to be valid in the way that the Qur'an is. Thus, the veracity of works and reports on the life of the Prophet, his actions, and his sayings vary widely. Muslim scholars have established methods and means with which to understand the Sunnah and their interpretation. It should be highlighted that the consensus is that any reported action of the Prophet Muhammad cannot contradict Qur'anic teachings and, by extension, the ethical refinement of prophetic character. This is especially important because it is understood that there are many things attributed to the life of Muhammad that are not valid. Additionally, when considering the Sunnah of the Prophet, there are those who interpret the Sunnah literally and consider the same *material* as essential, while others look at the intent and spirit of the Sunnah and how they would materialize today.

WHAT ARE HADITH?

The words of the Prophet Muhammad hold a special place for Muslims. A hadith is a saying of the Prophet. These words of the Prophet are transmitted in a number of well-known and studied books. The scholarly study of hadith is one of the most important Islamic disciplines and includes a methodology for analyzing the truthfulness of these sayings. Shi'a Muslims also extend the sayings of the Prophet's family, the Ahlul Bayt, into the larger category of narrations. They consider the sayings of the Ahlul Bayt to be explications and transmissions of Prophetic sayings. According to the Qur'an, the Prophet does not speak from a personal desire or selfishness. His words are not the Qur'an, since that is divine revelation, but rather they are inspired and informed by the Qur'an and sacred insight. It is important to note that Muslims make a clear distinction between the Qur'an as divine revelation and the hadith as words or sayings attributed to the Prophet. Scholars are in agreement that there are different classifications of hadith gathered in various collections and books. Among them are books that are considered more reliable than others. But there is no collection of hadith that can be taken uncritically. There are also shorter collections of selected hadith. Very popular in this category are collections of 40 hadith. Some hadith that have been narrated from the Prophet include the following:

- The one who has no love has no religion.

- The best of you in faith are the best in moral traits.

- Be merciful to others and you will receive mercy. Forgive others and God will forgive you.

- The Prophet was asked, "Whom is most loved by God?" He replied, "The one who benefits people the most."

- God is beautiful and loves beauty.

- Cleanliness is half of faith.

- Pray as if it is your last prayer.

- A man who fills his stomach while his neighbor is hungry is not a believer.

- Love is my foundation.

- You will not enter paradise until you believe, and you will not believe until you love each other. Shall I tell you about something if you do it, you will love each other? Spread peace among you.

- I have been sent to perfect beautiful ethical traits.

HOW ARE THE HADITH INTERPRETED?

In the analysis of hadith literature, scholars have a number of classifications for these reports. Thus, some hadith are considered valid, others as weak, and many others are invalid and fictional. Hadith scholarship considers a number of matters, including the chain of transmission or a study of how the hadith was disseminated. The personality and life of the individual narrating the hadith are scrutinized to see whether they can be considered truthful, and scholars are also probing the types of narrations that have been transmitted to determine whether they are historically sound. In addition to the chain of transmission, the actual content of the sayings attributed to Muhammad are also reviewed. Does the content agree with the Qur'an? Does it align with verified literature about the life and character of the Prophet and how he lived? In short, there are important ways to study and interpret narrations.

There are multiple books that have gathered narrations attributed to the Prophet. Many of these books are available in English translation. Muslims continue to publish books that include selected narrations as well as commentary on them.

Shari'a Defined

Islam views itself not only as a social and communally inclined religion but also as one that is one centered in a moral motivation. The individual and, by extension, the community are to be engaged, active, and mindful of moral activity as a spiritual obligation. The Shari'a is thus a very important aspect of Islamic teachings. The term "shari'a" can be translated as "the path leading to water."

Islamic teachings incorporate water in practical and theoretical aspects—water purifies both literally and figuratively. It is also the source of life. Thus, the Shari'a is both the determination of practical laws that are morally binding and a purifying agent that ensures spiritual readiness and growth for Muslims. The laws of Islam came to be codified under the Shari'a and in turn form one of the most important scholarly and communal undertakings for Muslims.

What Is Islamic Law?

The Shari'a is formulated by scholars who study Islamic jurisprudence (*fiqh*). These scholars specialize in a number of fields and undergo extensive training. The rulings of Shari'a utilize various sources for their decisions. These include the Qur'an, the verified sayings and life of the Prophet, reason, analogy, and scholarly consensus. The Shari'a is concerned with human activity. This includes daily prayers, charity contributions, marriage and divorce, inheritance, business transactions, food, and many other matters. The Shari'a is by nature pluralistic and considers social norms and customs when arriving at legal conclusions. There are certain objectives and aims of the Shari'a, but tangible, present, sociopolitical-economic considerations for the community are also considered. Moreover, Muslims who become expert jurists, or *mujtahid*, have independence in their legal conclusions. As long as their method is sound and aligns with the science of jurisprudence, their conclusion is valid. This points to the presence of differences in opinion among jurists, both historically and in present times. This is important to note: Since Shari'a is not in the hands of one person or entity, it is an active, plural, and morally bound endeavor.

The Shari'a may return results in several categories beyond binary right and wrong. These are:

OBLIGATORY

RECOMMENDED

INDIFFERENT
(neither sinful nor of any particular merit)

REPREHENSIBLE
(better to avoid, but not in the category of sin)

FORBIDDEN

These categories form different aspects of consideration when dealing with the various matters in which the Shari'a is involved. In other words, the Shari'a is broad in its scope and informed by multiple angles and fundamental matters that encompass multiple areas beyond the act itself. For example, brushing your teeth before daily prayers is recommended. But praying in clothing that has been purchased with unlawful income or means invalidates the prayer and is forbidden.

The Shari'a informs Muslims of their spiritual-ethical responsibilities. It considers the individual and the wider community as obligated to a set of morally bound rules derived from recognized sources. Thus, the marriage of a Muslim couple is guided by Shari'a. Offering physical assistance or financial aid to someone in need is also defined by Shari'a. The same goes for deciding on what should and should not be eaten. The Shari'a is an integral part of the identity and daily practice for committed

Muslims, and it informs their understanding of what it means to be a morally bound Muslim.

ROLE OF IMAMS

In Islam, a religious leader is known as an imam, but the role of a religious leader within the religion differs from the other monotheistic faiths. Islam does not have an institutional hierarchy like the Catholic church or other similar institutions. The degree and qualifications of religious leaders can vary. Not every imam is an expert jurist, and they may vary in their preference related to interpretive methods. One may be more literal, while another is mystically inclined, and so forth.

Imams also help promote Islamic scholarship. There are Muslim scholars whose qualifications, piety, scholarly acumen, and research stand out in the Islamic world, and imams will incorporate such scholarship in their local instruction. These individuals become sources of reference and authority for other scholars and by extension regular Muslims—either directly or indirectly—as a result of imams.

At a local level, imams lead congregational prayers, give sermons, and teach the community in areas ranging from the proper reading of the Qur'an in Arabic to Islamic mysticism and ethics. They also act as counselors and mediators in personal and family disputes, and they perform marriage ceremonies and burials. In the United States imams support enhanced engagement and outreach with the wider community and interfaith efforts.

ISLAMIC LAW AROUND THE WORLD

The formation of modern nation-states has shifted the Shari'a, welding it with secular and civil law. Most Muslim-majority countries have a formal affirmation of the presence of Shari'a law; however, the degree to which Shari'a is actually followed varies. Shari'a is not an isolated practice. It is engaged with other fields of knowledge, which inform Shari'a rulings.

For example, at the time of writing this book, the COVID-19 pandemic was wreaking global havoc. How does the Shari'a deal with such a pandemic? Even though congregational prayers are such an integral part of Islamic spiritual practice, as is the hajj pilgrimage, mosques were among the first institutions to suspend public gatherings. This decision was due to the prioritization of the views of medical experts and specialists in the field with the understanding that public gatherings increase the spread of disease. Thus, Shari'a can concurrently emphasize its obligation to public safety and well-being within the context of Islamic practice.

In non-Muslim countries, Muslims are bound by the Shari'a to follow civil law, unless it is unjust or in contradiction to Islamic teachings. For example, traffic laws, paying taxes, adhering to safety codes governing workplaces, and other similar civil laws must be followed. However, although alcohol is readily available for purchase, the Shari'a prohibits the consumption of alcohol. Muslims choose not to drink alcohol as a religiously informed decision.

CHAPTER 7

Culture and Daily Life

Though Islam emphasizes the idea of a unified collective of believers (ummah), Muslims are not monolithic. The opposite is the case. Varying interpretations of Islamic teaching can be found in the Muslim world, whether in law, philosophy, theology, family, culture, or daily life. Such diversity is integral to the intellectual and cultural history of Muslims. A narration attributed to prophet Muhammad states, "differences in opinion is a mercy to my nation." This chapter introduces some of these issues and views.

MUSLIM POPULATIONS AROUND THE WORLD

Muslim % of Total Population

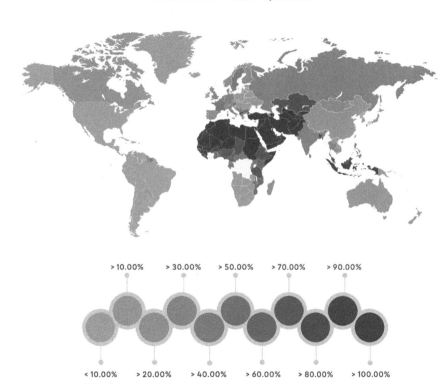

Data: Pew Research, 2009

Family and Individual Rights

Islamic teachings maintain extensive discourses on individual, family, and communal rights. These categories of individual, family, and society are considered to be interconnected both practically and spiritually. Islam offers teachings and guidance on ways of proper living deemed to be aligned with Islamic spiritual objectives.

FAMILY AND CHILDREN

The family unit is of utmost importance in Islamic teachings. Numerous Qur'anic verses and sayings of the Prophet emphasize the need for honoring, caring for, and serving parents. In reading the Qur'an, it becomes clear that Islam requires the relationship with parents to be informed by a specific virtue, ihsan. Ihsan can be understood as beautiful conduct, kindness, and goodwill. (Examples from the Qur'an include 2:83, 4:36, and 46:15.) This is even more pronounced when referring to mothers and motherhood. A hadith states, "Heaven lies beneath the feet of mothers." In yet another famous verse of the Qur'an, believers are commanded in such terms regarding parents:

> *If either or both of them reach old age with you, say no word that shows impatience with them, and do not be harsh with them, but speak to them respectfully and lower your wing in humility toward them in kindness*

and say, "Lord, have mercy on them, just as they cared for me when I was little." Your Lord knows best what is in your heart. If you are good, He is most forgiving to those who return to Him. **(The Qur'an 17:23–25)**

Islam emphasizes the need for emotional, spiritual, and material harmony within the home. The home is considered a sanctified space and impactful on the spiritual and human development of Muslims. Any kind of abuse or violence against children or a spouse is considered sinful and subject to punishment or fine under the Shari'a. Many aspects that may be considered ordinary or nonreligious take a spiritual hue through Islamic teachings. For example, earning an income through honest work to provide for one's family is considered worship, as is playing with children or smiling with one another. A Muslim husband and wife lovingly gazing at one another or feeding one another, for example, results in angels praying for the couple. Of special importance are teachings around the upbringing of children, especially with regard to religion, ethical behavior, and kindness. Islamic teaching emphasizes conflict resolution both inside and outside of the home. There is also a large amount of literature around the impact and power of prayers that parents, especially mothers, make for their children. This is considered a very spiritually sacred and productive prayer.

INHERITANCE

The Shari'a includes rules regarding exactly what and how much is inherited by surviving family members of the deceased. In some instances the rule allows for a male to receive more than a female, but this is not an absolute rule. Under Islamic law, the financial responsibility of the household falls in the hands of the men. Women may choose to contribute, but technically, it is not required. For this reason, the financial costs that men bear would be greater than women, hence, male heirs were traditionally favored. Muslims are highly encouraged to write wills as both a practical matter and to avert discord within the family.

MARRIAGE AND DIVORCE

A well-known narration attributed to Muhammad states, "Marriage is half of your religion." Islam places emphasis on the role and purpose of marriage and encourages Muslims toward it. A commonly recited verse in the Qur'an says: "Another of His signs is that He created spouses from among yourselves for you to live with in tranquility: He ordained love and kindness between you. There truly are signs in this for those who reflect" (The Qur'an 30:21).

The verse figures prominently in the Islamic wedding ceremony, the *nikah*, and displays a number of essential points within the Islamic conception of marriage, namely:

- God has created mates and partners for humans
- The three pillars for the creation and realization of this sign:
  - Tranquility
  - Love
  - Kindness

In other words, in order for the partnership to succeed, these characteristics must flourish and be maintained by the couple. Traditional Islamic teachings emphasize the responsibility of the husband to financially provide for the household. They also highlight the spiritual and intellectual rights of women, noting that men and women are created from the same essence (The Qur'an 4:1).

Under Islamic law, women have the right to pursue knowledge, work, own property, and inheritance. However, a wife is not required to spend her income on the upkeep of the family unless she chooses to. This is seen as granting independence to the wife within Islamic marriage. Additionally, the bride is given a *mahr* (bridal gift) by the groom—this can be monetary or non-monetary, according to the bride's preference.

The husband, on the other hand, has a religious obligation to work and provide for the family. In Islam, the husband and wife play an active role in complementing both the worldly and spiritual aspects of their development. Islamic teachings encourage procreation and raising children for those physically able to do so. Additionally, parents are tasked with ensuring the intellectual, emotional, and spiritual well-being of their children.

The Qur'an places great importance on family, in particular to maintaining respect, caring for family members, and being good to parents. This is highlighted in a number of verses. (For examples, see The Qur'an 4:36; 4:62; 17:23.) However, the role and appreciation of the mother outweighs that of the father. Narrations such as "Heaven lies beneath the feet of mothers" are ubiquitous in Muslim culture and discourse. The preservation of spiritually healthy and happy families is noted within

Islamic teachings. Divorce does take place within Muslim societies, but Islam views divorce as a last resort and it is looked down upon. Mediation, counseling, and reconciliation for couples to lessen or resolve disagreements and discord is preferred. In instances where divorce is necessary, there is a formal process conducted by a Muslim scholar.

POLYGAMY

Both historically and in modern times, polygamy has not been widely practiced throughout the Muslim world. Polygamy was a common practice in Arabia during the seventh century CE. As Islam spread, polygamy underwent a process of transformation among Arabs. Islam allows for polygamy, but with certain requirements, such as a restriction on the number of wives per husband. This represents a shift from the pre-Islamic precedent that placed no restrictions on the number of wives a man may have. Although polygamy is an option within Islam, it is not a general recommendation. Marriage between two people is preferred.

The Qur'an discusses polygamy in verse 3 of chapter 4, *The Women*. Early on, the verse mentions that marriage may be entered into with up to four women, unless one fears that they cannot be just and equitable, then only one. Polygamy is allowed under specific conditions such as the approval of the other partner and the guarantee that justice and equity in both emotional and material investment is upheld.

According to Muslim scholarship, the Prophet Muhammad married more than one woman because of political circumstances. Given the tribal nature of Arabia during the life of Muhammad, marriage was a way to build coalition and peace between tribes. The aim of these marriages was to build protective unions for the growing Muslim community. The Prophet's first marriage was to an older divorcée named Khadija. He did not marry a second time until Khadija had passed away and he was in old age. A sizeable percentage of Muslim men were killed in battles against the Meccan rulers and their affiliated tribes. The presence of widows and orphans, plus other female converts to Islam, created a need to provide protection and support. In these exceptional circumstances Muslim men were allowed to have more than one wife.

WOMEN'S RIGHTS IN ISLAM

Islamic textual teachings state that men and women are spiritually and temporally equal and that sin and spiritual reward is not different for one or the other. Women play essential roles in Islamic intellectual and cultural traditions as scholars, leaders, thinkers, and artists. Muslims cite the traditional example of the Prophet's wife Khadija as a source of support and comfort for the Prophet, who utilized her wealth to support the emerging Muslim community, freed slaves, and help the cause of Islam. Pre-Islamic Arabian society viewed women as second-class citizens and femicide (the killing of women and girls, especially by burying newborn girls) was practiced. Today, there are many examples of the success and vibrancy of Muslim women in all fields of life, especially in the United States.

Muslims believe that the pursuit of knowledge is incumbent upon every woman and man, equally.

In many Muslim-majority and -minority countries, women have access to education, spiritual development, gainful employment, safety in movement, and protection against abuse. Women are not required to adopt their husband's last name. Women have rights to property ownership, independence in deciding who to marry, and freedom to use their wealth. Moreover, under Islamic law, women have a right to demand monetary payment for things such as housework, raising children, and even breastfeeding a child.

DEATH

"Human beings are asleep, when they die, they will awaken." This famous hadith communicates both the inevitability of death and its result.

The individual is granted the opportunity to live in order to exhibit and achieve "the most virtuously beautiful manner" (The Qur'an 18:7). Islam considers that many individuals have not *awoken* to the reality of life. They are in a state of sleep—*the sleep of unawareness*. Once they die, they will realize that they did not understand the reality and purpose of life, but it will be too late.

Muslims believe that, with death, they will enter another realm of existence on the journey to the hereafter. Muslim rituals are very detailed when dealing with death and dying. Islamic teachings emphasize that one should not fear death, but they should remember it and righteously prepare for the afterlife. Only when a Muslim has not lived in a virtuous manner should they fear death. Additionally, Islam affirms that Muslims should not get attached to worldly life because it is fleeting. It is fine and recommended to enjoy life and be thankful for its blessings, but life should be understood as just one stage in the spiritual journey.

At death, a Muslim is to be ritually washed and shrouded. The body is then buried in a formal process that includes special prayers and steps for burial. Muslims do not believe in cremation and maintain that the body must be buried in a relatively quick time frame. Islam emphasizes the responsibility of praying for those who have passed on, and Muslims are encouraged to attend the funeral and burial of other Muslims. Common funeral prayers ask forgiveness and mercy for parents, relatives, and Muslims in general. To understand the full implications of this activity among Muslims, consider that at any moment a Muslim is praying for someone they don't know but consider to be a member of the Muslim community.

Lastly, visiting graveyards is highly recommended in Islam. It serves as an opportunity not only to pray for the deceased and keep their memory alive but also to remind oneself of the reality of death and thus increase spiritual activity and commitment while still alive. The Qur'an states that "every soul will taste death" (The Qur'an 21:35). Death is considered a new chapter and not the termination of human existence. The body is temporary, but the soul remains.

Economics

Economics and financial regulation have both worldly and spiritual aspects, according to Islam. The economy is central to maintaining the material functions of society. However, what should the aims and foundations of such a system be? Are they to be left to human desires and markets, or is there an ethical component and underpinning to economics in Islam? A unique set of rules related to financial practices, transactions, and labor exist in Islam. Work is considered a spiritual endeavor and an economy that serves the interests and needs of the population is essential to the spiritual and material well-being of the Muslim community. Islam strongly criticizes certain economic practices that contradict Islamic aims and ideals. Islamic economic theory is concerned with not just the basic functions of economics but a system dedicated to socioeconomic justice.

EARNING INTEREST

Interest is considered unlawful in Islam. Loans and credit exist in Muslim society, but loans are interest free. This ensures that the borrower does not get trapped in greater debt as a result of interest rates. Such usurious practices are considered predatory, un-Islamic, and a great sin. However, any natural increase in a person's wealth via work or investment is not an issue. The Qur'an states: "God deprives usurious gains of all blessing, whereas He blessed charitable deeds with manifold increase. And God does not love anyone who is stubbornly ingrate and persists in sinful ways" (The Qur'an: 2:276).

For Muslims living in the West, Islamic law allows them to take a loan for essential purchases, such as a house or a car, if they are unable to purchase them with cash. However, it is still better for the community to offer interest-free loans to members in order to avoid interest-based debt. Islamic teachings also sharply criticize extravagance and excess as well as the squandering of wealth. Moderation and contentment are highly valued and recommended traits.

BANKING AND LENDING SYSTEMS

Islamic banking has a number of considerations that incorporate a refusal of usury, avoidance of speculation, mutual agreement, clarity of terms between parties, and a requirement to engage only in ethical fields and industries. There are a growing number of Shari'a-compliant financial institutions in the United States that offer nonpredatory loans and investment portfolios. At a local level, Muslim communities utilize traditional methods of intercommunal lending as much as possible.

Food and Drink

The consumption of food and drink is a natural aspect of human sustenance. Islam considers food and drink as a direct link between the body, the spirit, and the ethical requirements of a spiritual life. Islamic teachings from a variety of sources (such as the Qur'an, hadith, and jurisprudence) illustrate the system of dietary laws in Islam. The method and meaning of this system is an important aspect of Islamic law. It also deals with the issue of humanity's relation to other animals and the environment.

Islam allows for the consumption of certain animals, but not others. In Muslim communities the production of and accessibility to Islamically sanctioned meat and other products is ubiquitous. Items approved for consumption under Islamic dietary law are referred to as halal. The list of halal animals includes beef, chicken, and fish (such as salmon, trout, tuna, etc.). The method of slaughtering sanctioned animals has a number of requirements, including the recitation of God's name, which is considered essential and has a purifying effect. There is further emphasis on the cleaning of the animal and removal of blood. Islamic law takes into account how animals are treated, and abuse of animals is prohibited.

Islamic teachings maintain that what Muslims eat impacts their heart and character. Thus, Muslims strive to maintain dietary guidelines as part of their spiritual practice. Any item or act that is prohibited and not halal is referred to as *haraam*, or forbidden. Islamic law considers pigs to be ritually impure and not appropriate for human consumption; additionally, predatory animals—such as sharks, tigers, and bottom-feeders from the ocean—are considered haraam.

Islamic teachings also maintain certain decorum regarding food, such as washing hands before and after eating and saying "Bismillah" (meaning "In the name of God") before a meal. It is important to chew food slowly, refrain from overeating, and to give thanks to God when finishing a meal.

HALAL

In the United States, access to halal food was limited in the
past. However, in the last few decades there has been a prolif-
eration of suppliers, restaurants, and other sources that meet
the needs of Muslim citizens. Additionally, the popularity of
cuisines from Muslim countries as well as restaurants that offer
halal burgers, pizza, sandwiches, etc. have introduced a large
number of non-Muslim Americans to Muslim cuisine and halal
food. A quick online search will now result in a large number of
halal options in most major US cities.

However, with the increase in the accessibility of halal
food, new challenges arise. How do Muslims ensure the ethical
requirements of halal in a globalized marketplace? There are
also concerns about the necessity of maintaining or reviv-
ing other traditional approaches to food and practices that
emphasize a good relationship with the land and the natural
environment, while discouraging wasteful consumption. Issues
such as a deteriorating climate and the environmental effects
of mass food production are intimately linked to the deeper
Islamic teachings about the reach, responsibilities, and limits of
humanity.

ALCOHOL AND DRUGS

The Qur'an and prophetic teachings prohibit the consumption of all types of alcohol. According to Islam, drinking any
amount of alcohol is sinful. Alcohol is viewed as socially and
spiritually destructive. The same can be said regarding Islamic

teachings on drugs. Recreational and experimental drug use is not allowed in Islam. A number of Muslim scholars also include smoking in the category of banned substances. However, if someone has a valid medical issue that requires the use of, for example, medical marijuana, exceptions are made.

Human beings are responsible for spiritual activity and refinement as well as their own physical health and well-being. Most Muslim-majority countries do not allow public sale or consumption of alcohol. Some Muslims drink alcohol; however, this is not a religiously sanctioned act. Moreover, Islamic teachings prohibit gambling. The Qur'an states: "O you of informed faith, intoxicants and gambling, idolatrous practices, and [divining with] arrows [a pagan Arab custom] are repugnant acts—Satan's doing—shun them so that you may prosper" (The Qur'an: 5:90).

Festivals and Holidays

The discussion on food and dietary consumption in Islam naturally leads to the topic of holidays and festivals—is there any holiday or festival without special food? There are a number of holidays and celebrations that are observed by Muslims. The Arabic word for festival is *eid*. In addition to shared holidays celebrated by all Muslims, there also are local and cultural celebrations such as the spring equinox (*Nowruz*) and many others. The two most prominent celebrations in the Muslim world are Eid al-Fitr and Eid al-Adha. Each of these celebrations is observed for three days. They include special congregational prayers, a sermon, and special alms donations. Narrations regarding all festivals mention that they are times of joy, celebration, and praise of God. It is also mentioned that any day that a Muslim spends in obedience to God and performing righteous deeds is an eid.

Eid is observed in Muslim culture in various ways, depending on the region and people. These include baking of special meals and sweets; wearing new clothes; visiting relatives, friends, and the community; as well as giving money or treats to kids. In the United States, many mosques have special bazaars during an eid, as well as picnics and games.

EID AL-FITR

The completion of the fast of Ramadhan is marked by the celebration of Eid al-Fitr. This celebration notes the success of dedicating and orienting oneself through fasting and other spiritual acts during Ramadhan in order to arrive at a more God-conscious state of being. As much as Eid al-Fitr is an occasion of celebration, it is also bittersweet for many Muslims as it marks the end of a month of heightened spiritual presence that they genuinely love and enjoy.

EID AL-ADHA

The second prominent holiday is linked with God's testing of the Prophet Abraham when he is informed that he will need to sacrifice his beloved son, the Prophet Ismail. This event, which is also one of the rites of the hajj pilgrimage, symbolizes complete devotion and sacrifice in the way of God. There are many works that detail the reasons why Abraham was tested with such an intense trial (although in the end Ismail is spared).

The Qur'an mentions the occurrence in the following verse: "'O my son! I have seen in a dream that I offer you in sacrifice, now what is your view?' The son said, 'O my father! Do as you are commanded, you will find me to be one of the steadfast if God so wills'" (The Qur'an 37:102). To mark this festival, Muslims sacrifice an animal—usually a sheep or lamb—and distribute the meat, particularly to the needy. The sacrifice of the animal is intended to convey the killing of the ego.

OTHER CELEBRATIONS

The celebration of the birth of the Prophet Muhammad is another major occasion in Islamic spirituality. These celebrations include the recitation of special supplications, poetry, songs, and speeches about the life and character of the Prophet. Celebrations marking the birth of other members of the Prophet's family, as well as saints, are also common in the Muslim world. Shi'a Muslims in particular also celebrate the occasion of Ghadir Khum—when the Prophet is reported to have declared Ali the leader of the Muslim community.

Dress Codes

Islamic teachings emphasize modest clothing for men and women. Islam has a philosophy around interactions between and among genders, and proximity is delineated based on sanctioned relations between individuals. In regular interactions and social settings, a Muslim's character, intelligence, and skills should be prominent, not their bodily form. The body is considered sacred and not to be exposed to the general public. Additionally, modest clothing is viewed as constructive toward a society that restricts physical temptation and objectification. These teachings on modest dress are generally materialized in modest attire based on local history. Muslims everywhere are mandated to dress well and maintain good appearance. This emphasis focuses on cleanliness, upkeep, and modest adornment.

Muslim women wear attire that does not expose cleavage or the chest or legs and moves attention away from the curvature of the body. Moreover, many Muslim women wear a head scarf (*hijab*) to cover their hair. This is viewed as a sign of modesty and devotion to God. The style of hijab can vary from place to place or even within the same country.

In addition to modest dress, Muslims also place as much, or arguably more, emphasis on modesty in action. This includes avoiding flaunting the body and material possessions as well as lowering the gaze to evade objectifying or lusting after the opposite sex. Islam looks at the human form as sacred and considers humankind to have been created in the best of forms.

All types of verbal harassment, catcalling, and lewd comments are considered un-Islamic. There has been an increase in the popular reception and prominence of modest Muslim fashion online and by large retailers. There are numerous Muslim entrepreneurs who have fashion businesses providing items ranging from head scarves to caftans, T-shirts, dresses, and traditional attire (which normally tend to be less formfitting). Moreover, the ethical production and treatment of workers who produce clothing is an important ethical component in Islamic attire.

VARIATIONS ON MODEST DRESS

Converts to Islam

Islam is the world's fastest-growing religion both as a result of natural birth and through conversions. Any individual who chooses to embrace Islam can become Muslim by simply reciting the Declaration of Faith (shahadah). Islam views conversion in a positive light and as a personal decision. An individual cannot be forced to become Muslim. This notion is contradictory to the Islamic ethos since the choice of religion has been left to the individual. If choice was irrelevant, Muslims assert, God would have denied humankind the will to decide on whether to believe or disbelieve in religion. In the words of, the Qur'an, "There is no compulsion in religion" (2:256).

In the United States, all sorts of people from different backgrounds and stages of life embrace Islam. When any person decides to convert to Islam, they typically contact a local mosque or Islamic center. When they are ready, the imam of the mosque or any other Muslim can accompany them in reciting the Declaration of Faith: "I bear witness that there is no god but God, and I bear witness that Muhammad is God's servant and messenger."

Once this declaration is made, they are recognized as Muslim. Additionally, Muslims believe that all of their past sins and shortcomings are forgiven at this moment. Islamic teachings maintain that new converts have a fresh slate before God and benefit from a unique mercy of God, who guided them to Islam. The imam and community members will work with the convert as they learn to perform the daily prayers and grow in their practice of Islam. The mosque's imam and community members will spend time helping new converts in their transition to an Islamic lifestyle; give them books they can read; assist in the memorization of Qur'anic verses; and give them gifts such as a prayer rug, rosary beads, scarves (for women), traditional caps (for men), or other items. This is to welcome the individual within the local community and to emphasize the notion of membership in the wider, unified, global collective of Muslims.

Some mosques or Islamic community centers also offer general classes on Islam that can be attended by all local community members. With the increase in the number of Muslim converts in the United States, there are also a number of convert support groups and organizations. Someone who converts to Islam does not have to change their name. However, some Muslim converts do decide to adopt a new name to complete the transition if they deem it necessary.

CHAPTER 8

Relationship to Judaism and Christianity

Contrary to what some may think, three of the world's most prominent religions, Judaism, Christianity, and Islam, hold many things in common. Naturally, there are a number of differences between them, but they have become collectively known as the Abrahamic religions or faiths, as they share a common belief that their shared heritage arises from the ancient story of Abraham. This chapter will offer readers insight on the similarities and differences between the Abrahamic faiths, as well as the ways to and possibilities for a more peaceful coexistence. It is pivotal to distinguish the traditional approaches and scholarly views on this topic from those coming from fringe elements. In a post-9/11 world, interfaith outreach and programming between the Abrahamic traditions has helped defuse tension. These efforts toward peace and cooperation from religious leaders, institutions, and general practitioners of the faith offer a lot of context on the reach and limits of such practices. At a time of increasing fractures and fissures in US society, many faith leaders are emphasizing the centrality of interfaith relations and mutual understanding between the Abrahamic faiths and beyond.

Holy Books

One of the primary similarities between the Abrahamic faiths is the central presence of a holy book. The Qur'an has numerous references to other revelations and thus expands the sphere of revelation and revelatory presence beyond the Qur'an.

The Qur'an speaks of the holy books of Jews and Christians—the Tawraat (Torah) and Injeel (Gospel), revealed to Moses and Jesus, respectively. Islam categorizes Jews and Christians as *Ahl al-Kitab*, or People of the Book. Muslims believe Jews and Christians received a book of revelation through Moses and the life of Jesus, though they understand that process as different from the revelation of the Qur'an to Muhammad. In other words, it serves as a direct reference to the Islamic belief in divine revelation. From the Qur'an:

Truly, We revealed the Torah in which was guidance and light. **(The Qur'an 5:44)**

And we sent after them in their footsteps Isa (Jesus), Son of Maryam (Mary), verifying what was before him of the Tawraat (Torah) and We gave him the Injeel (Gospel) in which was guidance and light. **(The Qur'an 5:46)**

In addition to the previous instances of recognition of the Torah and Gospel and the presence of the category of People of the Book, the Qur'an calls for engagement and cooperation between the faiths:

Say, "People of the Book, let us arrive at a statement that is common to us all: we worship God alone, we ascribe no partner to Him, and none of us takes others beside God as lords." If they turn away, say, "Witness our devotion to Him." **(The Qur'an: 3:64)**

THE TORAH, THE BIBLE, AND THE QUR'AN: SIMILARITIES

There are a number of noteworthy things shared among the Abrahamic faiths. The primary belief of the three faiths is of a singular God—monotheism. Of course, the details vary, but the centrality of this principle is essential in each faith. Further similarities include the creation of Adam and Eve, the existence and purpose of prophecy, and doing good works and offering charity. Moreover, the texts emphasize the presence of sin, both past and present, and highlight the need for God's forgiveness and mercy. Many of the prophets of the Old Testament are also noted in the Qur'an. These include the prophets Aaron, Adam, Abraham, Noah, and Job. Narratives from the lives of the prophets are mentioned in these holy accounts, shared by the three faiths: Moses and Pharaoh, the splitting of the sea, Noah's Ark, and Jonah, as well as many others.

The holy books of Islam and Judaism have similar systems of dietary laws. The terms kosher and halal share a common meaning and usage in reference to that which is allowed or suitable for consumption or action. Furthermore, the Lord's Prayer in Christianity can be understood as akin to the far-reaching presence of al-Fatiha, the first chapter of the Qur'an. Although the language and words of the three holy books may be different, the spirit and aim can be understood to be similar and shared. Each of the religions shares within their texts similar codes of conduct, such as avoiding hypocrisy and not making offerings to idols. They extol the importance of being humble before God, putting trust in God, helping the needy, and repentance. The holy books also warn of the folly in disobedience to God.

THE TORAH, THE BIBLE, AND THE QUR'AN: DIFFERENCES

Although, many common themes are present in the Abrahamic religions, there are differences between the three faiths. There are also areas where there is agreement between Islam and Christianity on a given matter but a divergence with Judaism on the same topic. Similarly, there are instances in which Islam and Judaism are more aligned on a matter and Christianity differs in viewpoint. Examples of this are the existence of Jesus and his miraculous birth, both accepted by Muslims and Christians but disputed by Judaism.

A defining characteristic of Islamic monotheism as expressed through the Qur'an is its absolute quality. Islam considers God's power as active and immediately involved in the current world. God's absolute authority (tawhid) rejects any notion that God's omnipotence is limited or that God has begotten a son, as expressed in the Christian veneration of Jesus.

Another difference between the Qur'an and the other holy books centers on the concept of trust between God and humanity. The Qur'an asserts that before the creation of the world, God offered his trust (*amana*) first (The Qur'an 33:72). Islamic scholars have long contemplated the implications and reality of what this means. Common themes in that discussion include the issue of humanity's vice-regency on earth (The Qur'an 2:30 and 38:26) and the act of "knowing all the names" (The Qur'an 2:31), a reference to the unique capacity for reason and knowledge granted to humanity as related in the Qur'an. Additionally, the concept of amana may also encapsulate the notion of free will as discussed earlier in the book.

Although the Qur'an maintains that the Torah and Gospel were sent as "guidance and light," Islam believes that the Christian and Jewish holy books were subsequently altered, according to the Qur'an.

Jesus and Prophets

Islamic teachings assert that God selects prophets not just as examples of righteous believers but so that they can extend and invite others to the divine message. The selection of prophets is a divine act and cannot be determined or changed by humankind. As God's messengers, prophets invite people to the faith, engage in righteous deeds, and turn away from any aberration on the true path of God. Given that they are tasked with delivering God's message, Muslims believe prophets are infallible.

According to Islam, prophets are human but not ordinarily so. Prophets are spiritually and intellectually perfect. Islamic teachings mention that a large number of prophets were sent by God, and several narrations include that number as 124,000 or greater. Among the messengers of God, Islam holds certain prophets with a rank of special majesty: Abraham, Jesus, Moses, Muhammad, and Noah. The Qur'an states: "We favored some of these messengers above others. God spoke to some; others He raised in rank; We gave Jesus, son of Mary, Our clear signs and strengthened him with the holy spirit" (The Qur'an 2:253).

STATUS OF JESUS IN ISLAM

Islam considers Jesus as one of God's greatest prophets. Numerous verses in the Qur'an mention Jesus (Isa) and his exalted status. For Muslims, belief in prophets is one of the tenants of faith. The prophets mentioned in the Qur'an are of a special consideration, unique to Islam. Muslims are required not only to believe in the Qur'anic prophets, but to love and honor them. For this reason, when Muslims say, hear, or write the names of any of these prophets, they include "peace be upon him" with the name as an honorific.

The Qur'an recounts the miraculous birth of Jesus from the Virgin Mary (Maryam). Thus, when Jesus is mentioned in the Qur'an, he is mentioned as "Isa, son of Maryam." Multiple Qur'anic verses speak of his birth (especially 19:16–36). Moreover, there are references to his miracles. The Qur'an says that Jesus is blessed with peace from God, as well as counted among those who are *near* to God's mercy and grace. The Qur'an also mentions that Jesus spoke from the cradle and was sent as a messenger to the Children of Israel.

The references to Jesus within the Qur'an are many and comprehensive, with the differences centering on the following:

- Jesus is a prophet of God and not God or the son of God.

- The Qur'an explains the virgin birth through the lens of Adam and Eve, both created without any parents. When God decrees and intends something, God simply commands it. "In God's eyes Jesus is just like Adam: He created him from dust, said to him, 'Be,' and he was" (The Qur'an 3:59).

- Jesus noted that he is a prophet of God and gave "the good news of a prophet after me, his name is Ahmad" (The Qur'an 61:6). One of the names of the Prophet Muhammad is Ahmad.

- Jesus was not crucified and did not die for the sins of humanity. The Qur'an denies the crucifixion and states that he was raised to heaven and is alive without having been killed (The Qur'an 4:157).

In addition to Qur'anic verses such as, "Peace was on me the day I was born, and will be on me the day I die and the day I am raised to life again" (The Qur'an 19:33), there are numerous sayings attributed to Jesus in Islamic literature. One such attribution is the following: "The most wretched person is known for their knowledge and unknown for their deeds" ('Oddat al-Da'i, narration number 158).

ABRAHAM

Abraham is a central figure in the Qur'an and presented as an exemplary prophet and believer. His role in the construction of the Ka'ba and as the patriarch of subsequent prophets is of great importance to Muslims. He represents the employment of reason and contemplation in reaching the state of witnessing God's signs and an unwavering belief in God. (See especially 6:74.) Abraham is referred to as the Friend of God (The Qur'an 4:125), and multiple verses describe him as upright and in complete devotion to God: "Most surely Ibrahim was forbearing, tender-hearted, and devout" (The Qur'an 11:75).

Referring to Abraham in the genealogy of religion, the Qur'an states:

Abraham was neither a Jew nor a Christian. He was upright and devoted to God, never an idolater, and the people who are closest to him are those who truly follow his ways, this Prophet, and [true] believers—God is close to [true] believers. **(The Qur'an 3:67–68)**

The Qur'anic story of Abraham includes combating idolatry and the unjust rule of Nimrod. Abraham destroyed the idols worshipped by his people (21:51–73), and he was to be burned alive for this. The narrative of Abraham cast into the fire is of importance in Islamic mysticism and discourse. The Qur'an mentions that, "We said: O fire! Be cool and safe for Abraham" (The Qur'an 21:69).

ADAM AND EVE

The Qur'an refers to humankind as the Children of Adam. Adam's creation as the human archetype, alongside Eve, is central to the Genesis story common to Judaism, Christianity, and Islam. But, even though the story is a common theme between the three religions, there are a number of differences between Islamic teachings surrounding Adam and Eve and those of the Judeo-Christian tradition.

Islam teaches that Adam and Eve were created from the same essence (The Qur'an 4:1). The Qur'an does not state that Eve was created from Adam's rib cage, as is the case in Judaism and Christianity. The Tree of Knowledge, which Adam and Eve were warned not to approach in the Torah and Bible, does not appear in this way in the Qur'an. In Islamic teachings, knowledge is an essential facet of human sacred obligation. God teaches Adam, imparting knowledge (The Qur'an 2:31). Another difference is the cause of Adam and Eve's banishment from the garden. In the Qur'an, Eve alone is not blamed for this eviction. The verse places responsibility on both Adam and Eve. (See, for example, 2:36, 7:9–23, and 20:121.) Lastly, Islam views the banishment as a necessary stage in human development and its relationship with seeking the Divine. The Qur'an makes clear that it was God who taught Adam and Eve words to supplicate and beseech God for mercy and grace (see 2:37 and 7:23).

ORIGINAL SIN

Unlike Christianity, Islam and Judaism do not subscribe to the concept of original sin. Islam teaches that humans are born pure and sinless. As a result of the course of life, people become susceptible to sin and shortcomings; however, God's mercy and forgiveness are offered to those who repent, return to the righteous path, and strive to reform. Islam and Judaism also share the same notion of redemption. Christianity holds to a concept of redemption, but it is inseparable from the idea of original sin. Lastly, Islam emphasizes that each individual is responsible for their own actions and sins, but there is also a collective responsibility to help and remind one another of the ways of keeping to the spiritual path.

RELIGIOUS EXTREMISM

Islamic spirituality emphasizes the need for balance and equilibrium. The Qur'an says, "We have made you [believers] into a just community, so that you may bear witness [to the truth] before others and so that the Messenger may bear witness [to it] before you" (The Qur'an 2:143). However, we see a number of instances of religious extremism committed by Muslims. There is an unfortunate stereotype in the world that emphasizes religious extremism as something unique only to Islam, but an honest consideration of the history of religions, as well as a scan of contemporary events, shows that religious extremism exists among followers of all religions. Religious extremism and violence committed by Jews and Christians should not be used to paint all Jews and Christians as inclined to violence, and it should not be used to tar Muslims in the same way. One can study the upheaval and violence caused during the Crusades of the medieval period as a prime example of Christian religious intolerance and extremism, or the Ku Klux Klan, England's imperialist agenda in India and the Caribbean, and many other instances. Violence and murder caused by extremist Jews is also well documented in Israel. Hindu extremism and violence is also well documented and active in India. The United Nations recognized the concerted violence and terror in Myanmar by Buddhists as genocide. These are just a few examples exposing the destructive and tragic results of religious extremism. This can also extend to any kind of extremism and racism (such as the systematic oppression of African Americans and others), since violence is not unique to followers of religion.

When the underlying aims, background, and motivations of these groups and individuals are perused and studied, trends begin to appear that show the reasons why such forces use religion as a rallying cry. Religion has social currency. The actual aims of the groups are often much more political and tied to worldly aspirations.

Despite the prevalence of religious violence in history, nothing in the modern era has inflicted as much violence and destruction comparable to that wrought by nation-states and secular political ideologies. A brief study of the history of World War II, the rise of Communism in Russia and China, Pol Pot in Cambodia, or the American war in Vietnam illustrates the toll of state and ideological violence.

All traditional religions maintain the importance of peace and cooperation between human beings. The Qur'an mentions

If anyone kills a person—unless in retribution for murder or spreading corruption in the land—it is as if he kills all mankind, while if any saves a life it is as if he saves the lives of all mankind (5:32).

Religious extremists abuse and exploit religion as well as concoct deviant interpretations of sacred texts to justify their violence. They deny the very central aspect of mankind's shared humanity. From the perspective of mainstream religious teachings, extremists are deviant. It is of utmost importance for individuals of moral integrity and conviction to unite against the demonization of any religious group as uniquely responsible for violence and instead look at what the traditional scholarship and canonical teachings offer in order to better understand the teachings of that particular religion and combat the demonization and weaponization of violence against such groups.

Comparisons with Judaism and Christianity

Say, "People of the Book, let us arrive at a statement that is common to us all: we worship God alone, we ascribe no partner to Him, and none of us takes others beside God as lords." If they turn away, say, "Witness our devotion to Him." **(The Qur'an: 3:64)**

Islam teaches commonality with other religions and peoples. Of special consideration are Jews and Christians. Among the religions is a shared, though not uniform, understanding of belief in one God. In the realm of human actions, charity, forgiveness, and service to humankind are emphasized by these faiths as well. If an individual is looking to find commonalities and areas of agreement, many are present. However, if someone is focused on differences and in turn interprets those differences as sources of conflict, then that individual will also be busy. The main question is this: Are individuals looking for understanding, cooperation, and living in harmony with others, or are they seeking out disagreements, animosity, and conflict? Wherever we invest our energies and efforts, we will see an outcome. For peace, we should look for commonality.

INTERFAITH MOVEMENTS

One of the most promising and inspiring efforts is that of interfaith movements, which seek to broaden understanding between major religious groups. Such efforts have a multifaceted approach.

Knowing one another and gathering information on beliefs and practices directly from scholars and adherents of the faith.

Recognizing and highlighting similarities and shared ideals.

Combating Islamophobia and other sources of misinformation and its weaponization for violence both in the United States and abroad.

Committing to social justice and empowerment efforts to combat issues such as poverty, climate catastrophe, homelessness, antiwar efforts, and much more.

Interfaith projects are often described as deeply positive experiences by those who participate. Such opportunities present unique platforms for engagement. A Muslim imam might teach a lesson on Islamic faith and culture at a church, or a rabbi might speak about Jewish rites at an Islamic center or mosque. Interfaith programming revitalizes the recognition of the shared human experience and the beauty of compassion and communication. As the Qur'an attests:

> O mankind, we created you all from a single man and
> a single woman, and made you into races and tribes
> so that you get to know one another. In the sight of
> God, the noblest of you is the one who is most deeply
> conscious of Him: God is all knowing, all aware.
> **(The Qur'an 49:13)**

The Qur'an insists not on a mere recognition of differences but on reaching below the surface to actually get to *know* one another, to understand a shared reality, and to note that what truly sets the human being apart is righteous action, which is the direct result of God-consciousness. A maxim attributed to Imam Ali asserts, "People are of two kinds: either your equal in faith, or your equal in humanity" (Nahj al-Balagha, letter 53).

TOLERANCE OF RELIGIOUS MINORITIES

Islam forbids the persecution of religious minorities and individuals of other faiths. Individuals are offered peace and choice regarding their personal faith. Moreover, Islam recognizes the presence of other religions and belief systems. There are a number of sources that maintain this view. Qur'anic verses, such as, "There is no compulsion in religion" (2:256) and "You have your religion and I have mine" (The Qur'an 109:6), convey both the presence of other belief systems and the necessity of choice in adhering to religion. From the life of the Prophet Muhammad, examples such as the Charter of Madinah (discussed in chapter 3) as well as the presence of multiple belief systems in Madinah and Mecca prove that expressions of tolerance are possible. When Muhammad accepted the surrender of Meccans to the Muslim army, he forgave them and granted them safety. Violence against religious minorities or other religions is not taught in Islam. Islamic law requires that religious sites be preserved and not destroyed, even during armed conflict. Lastly, we see that throughout Islamic history, religious minorities have often lived in peaceful coexistence in Muslim societies. There are churches, temples, and synagogues throughout the Muslim world from Iran to Jordan, Egypt to Afghanistan.

GLOSSARY OF TERMS

Ablution: *wudhu*. Ritual washing of body parts for daily prayers and other acts.

Adhan: the Muslim call to prayer. Vocalized in a harmonized manner.

Ahl al-Kitab: People of the Book. A reference to Jews, Christians, Sabeans, and Zoroastrians.

Ahlul Bayt: the family of the Prophet Muhammad. Continues through his daughter, Fatima, and her husband, Ali. Certain members are considered to possess a unique spiritual status.

Allah: the Arabic term for God. The True Being.

Asma al-husna: The Most Beautiful Names. Refers to the *names* of God such as The Most Merciful, Just, Forgiving, etc.

Bismillah: the ubiquitous verse of the Qur'an: "In the Name of God, the all Compassionate, the especially Merciful."

Caliphate: the institution of political leadership after the passing of Prophet Muhammad.

Dhikr: to lovingly recall God. The practice of uttering names of God and prayers.

Eid: any one of the major Islamic holidays.

Hadith: sayings attributed to the Prophet Muhammad.

Hafez: the title of someone who has memorized the entire Qur'an. Derived from the verbs *safeguard* and *protect*.

Hajj: spiritual pilgrimage.

Hajji(a): a male (female) who has successfully completed the Muslim pilgrimage.

Halal: refers to what is allowed. Common reference to meat that is allowed under Islamic dietary law.

Haraam: refers to what is prohibited.

Hawa: Eve.

Hijrah: the migration of Muslims from Mecca to Madinah. Also marks the beginning of the Islamic calendar.

Iblis: the name for Satan in Islam.

Ibrahim: Abraham.

Ihram: the state of sanctity. When the pilgrim begins hajj processions.

Ihsan: virtuously beautiful action.

Injeel: gospel.

Insan: people; the forgetful being; the one in need of affinity. A reference to humans.

Iman: informed faith. Faith following effort and deliberation.

Imamate: belief that after the Prophet Muhammad, spiritual and political authority of the Muslims belongs to select members of his family, Ahlul Bayt.

Isa: Jesus.

Islam: surrender to peace or submission to the Will of God.

Jahiliyya: age of ignorance. A reference to the prevalent practices in pre-Islamic Arabia. Also any state of ignorance.

Jibrīl: Angel Gabriel.

Jihad: to exert effort, struggle, strive. A spiritual exercise and commitment to conquer the soul.

Ka'ba: the cube-shaped structure that is Islam's holiest site and the location for the annual pilgrimage, the hajj.

Madhab: school of thought. Refers to Shi'a and Sunni interpretations.

Madinah: formerly known as Yathrib, now *"City of the Prophet."* The city that the Prophet Muhammad migrated to and where he is buried.

Maryam: Mary. The mother of Jesus and considered one of the best creations of God. She is highlighted in the Qur'an for her piety.

Masjid: mosque. The place of worship, prayer, and instruction.

Mecca: a city in modern-day Saudi Arabia. Birthplace of Muhammad and site of the Ka'ba.

Muhammad: the Prophet of Islam. Considered to be the Final Prophet of God.

Muharram: the first month of the Islamic calendar. The month of mourning due to the martyrdom of the Prophet Muhammad's grandson, Imam Hussein, alongside his companions and members of the Prophet's family.

Musa: Moses.

Muslim: an individual who believes in the religion of Islam.

Nuh: Noah.

Qibla: the direction toward the Ka'ba for canonical prayers.

Qur'an: the holy book of Islam. Considered to be verbatim and unchanged revelation from God.

Rak'at: a unit of prayer (salat). Consists of standing, bowing, prostrating, and sitting, in addition to the recitation of the Qur'an and other verbal formulae.

Ramadhan: Islamic month of fasting.

Salat: prayer, especially the five canonical daily prayers.

Shahadah: the testimony of faith in Islam.

Shari'a: Islamic law. *"The path that leads to water."*

Sufism: *tasawwuf*. The mystical path of Islam. Focuses on esoteric interpretations and the purification of the heart.

Sunnah: deeds and actions attributed to the Prophet Muhammad.

Tawaf: circumambulation of the Ka'ba.

Taqwa: God-consciousness. Care and concern for God's law and religion.

Tawhid: the absolute Oneness of God. Belief and reliance upon God alone.

Tawraat: Torah.

Zakat: "purifying charity" offered by Muslims.

RECOMMENDED READING AND RESOURCES

Books

THE QUR'AN AND ITS INTERPRETATIONS

Haleem, M. A. *The Qur'ān: A new translation by M.A.S. Abdel Haleem* (New York: Oxford University Press, 2004).

Izutsu, Toshihiko. *Ethico-Religious Concepts in the Qur'ān* (Montreal: McGill-Queen's University Press, 2002).

Kermani, Navid. *God is Beautiful: The Aesthetic Experience of the Quran* (Medford: Polity, 2018).

Nasr, Sayyed Hossein, et al. *The Study Quran: A New Translation and Commentary* (New York: HarperOne, 2015).

Qarā'ī, 'Q. *The Qur'ān: With a phrase-by-phrase English translation* (Qum, The Centre for Translation of the Holy Qur'ān, 2015).

Shah-Kazemi, Reza. *Spiritual Quest: Reflections on Qur'ānic Prayer According to the Teachings of Imam 'Alī* (New York: I.B. Tauris, 2011).

MUHAMMAD

Cole, Juan. *Muhammad: Prophet of Peace Amid the Clash of Empires* (New York: Nation Books, 2018).

Considine, Craig. *The Humanity of Muhammad: A Christian View* (Clifton: Blue Dome Press, 2020).

Mohiuddin, Meraj. *Revelation: The Story of Muhammad* (Whiteboard Press, 2015).

HISTORY OF ISLAM AND ISLAMIC SCIENCES

Dakake, Maria Massi. *The Charismatic Community: Shi'ite Identity in Early Islam* (Albany: State University of New York Press, 2007).

Madelung, Wilferd. *The Succession to Muhammad: A Study of the Early Caliphate* (Cambridge: Cambridge University Press, 1977).

Mutahhari, Murtada. *Islamic Sciences: An Introduction* (London: Saqi Books, 2002).

Nasr, Seyyed Hossein. *The Heart of Islam: Enduring Values for Humanity* (New York: HarperOne, 2004).

Shah-Kazemi, Reza. *Imam 'Ali: From Concise History to Timeless Mystery* (London: Matheson Trust, 2019).

Sharī'atī, 'Ali. *Hajj: Reflection on Its Rituals* (Islamic Publications International, 1977).

MYTHS ABOUT ISLAM AND MUSLIMS

Ernst, Carl W. *Following Muhammad: Rethinking Islam in the Contemporary World* (Chapel Hill: University of North Carolina Press, 2003).

Ghazzālī, A. M., and J. R. Crook. J. R. *The Alchemy of Happiness* (Chicago: Great Books of the Islamic World, 2008).

Murata, Sachiko, and William C. Chittick. *The Vision of Islam* (New York: I.B. Tauris, 2006).

Rizvi, Sajjad H. *Mulla Sadra and Metaphysics: Modulation of Being* (New York: Routledge, 2009).

Safi, Omid. *Radical Love: Teachings from the Islamic Mystical Tradition* (New Haven: Yale University Press, 2018).

ISLAM IN THE UNITED STATES

Abd-Allah, Umar F. *A Muslim in Victorian America: The Life of Alexander Russell Webb* (Oxford: Oxford University Press, 2006).

Chan-Malik, Sylvia. *Being Muslim: A Cultural History of Women of Color in American Islam* (New York: New York University Press, 2018).

Hussain, Amir. *Muslims and the Making of America* (Waco, TX: Baylor University Press, 2016).

Selod, Saher. *Forever Suspect: Racialized Surveillance of Muslim Americans in the War on Terror* (New Brunswick: Rutgers University Press, 2018).

HADITH AND NARRATIONS

Al-Ḥusayn, S. A., M. Muṭahharī, and Y. T. Jibouri. *Nahjul Balagha - Peak of eloquence* (Elmhurst, NY: Tahrike Tarsile Qur'an, 2018).

Al-Nawawi, Y. *The 40 Hadith of Imam al-Nawawi* (Johannesburg: Lote Tree Press, 2018).

al-Qadi al-Quda'i. *Light in the Heavens: Sayings of the Prophet Muhammad.* Translated by Tahera Qutbuddin (New York: New York University Press, 2019).

Brown, Jonathan A. C. *Misquoting Muhammad: The Challenge and Choices of Interpreting the Prophet's Legacy* (London: Oneworld, 2014).

Ray'shahrī, M. Muhammadi. *The Scale of Wisdom: A Compendium of Shi'a Hadith.* Translated by N. Virjee, et al. (London: ICAS Press, 2009).

ISLAMIC INFLUENCE AROUND THE WORLD

Adib-Moghaddam, Arshin. *Metahistory of the Clash of Civilisation: Us and Them Beyond Orientalism* (Oxford: Oxford University Press, 2010).

Esmail, Aziz. *The Poetics of Religious Experience: The Islamic Context* (London: I.B. Tauris, 1998).

Murata, Sachiko. *Chinese Gleams of Sufi Light: Wang Tai-yu's Great Learning of the Pure and Real and Liu Chih's Displaying the Concealment of the Real Realm* (New York: SUNY Press, 2000).

Wang, D., and S. Murata. *The First Islamic Classic in Chinese: Wang Daiyu's Real Commentary on the True Teaching* (Albany: State University of New York Press, 2018).

ISLAMIC ART, ARCHITECTURE, AND LITERATURE

al-Busiri, Imam, et al. *The Mainstay: A Commentary on Qasida Al-Burda* (Keighley, Abu Zahra Press, 2015).

'Aṭṭār, F. A., D. Davis, and A. Darbandi. *The Conference of the Birds* (London, England: Penguin Books, 2011).

Burckhardt, Titus. *Art of Islam: Language and Meaning* (Bloomington: World Wisdom, 2009).

Hanash, Idham Mohammed. *The Theory of Islamic Art: Aesthetic Concept and Epistemic Structure* (Herndon: International Institute of Islamic Thought, 2017).

Rumi, Jalaluddin. *Signs of the Unseen: The Discourses of Jalaluddin Rumi*. Translated by W. M. Thackston Jr. (Boston: Shambhala, 1994).

Shaw, Wendy M. K. *What is "Islamic" Art?: Between Religion and Perception* (Cambridge: Cambridge University Press, 2019).

MUSLIMS' CONTRIBUTIONS TO SCIENCES AND PHILOSOPHY

al-Hassani, Salim. *1001 Inventions: The Enduring Legacy of Muslim Civilization: Official Companion to the 1001 Inventions Exhibition* (Washington, DC: National Geographic, 2012).

Meisami, Sayeh. *Nasir al-Din Tusi: A Philosopher for All Seasons* (Islamic Texts Society, 2019).

Morgan, Michael H. *Lost History: The Enduring Legacy of Muslim Scientists, Thinkers, and Artists* (Washington, DC: National Geographic, 2008).

Rashed, Roshdi. *Al-Khwarizmi: The Beginnings of Algebra* (London: Saqi Books, 2010).

ISLAM AND VIEWS ON WOMEN

Inloes, Amina. *Women in Shi'ism: Ancient Stories, Modern Ideologies* (Piscataway: Gorgias Press, 2019).

Schimmel, Annemarie. *My Soul Is a Woman: The Feminine in Islam* (New York: Continuum, 1997).

Tabataba'i, Allamah Muhammad Husayn. *Women in Islam*. Translated by Abuzar Ahmadi (Light of Islam Books, 2017).

Diouf, Sylviane A. *Servants of Allah: African Muslims Enslaved in the Americas* (New York: New York University Press, 1998).

Jackson, Sherman A. *Islam and the Blackamerican: Looking Toward the Third Resurrection* (Oxford: Oxford University Press, 2005).

Malcolm X, and Alex Haley. *The Autobiography of Malcolm X* (New York: Ballantine, 1964).

Websites

al-islam.org

imam-us.org

madinainstitute.com

zaytuna.edu

INDEX

A

Ablution, 36, 102
Abraham (prophet), 4, 51–52, 132–133, 146–147
Abu Bakr, 69, 72, 79–80
Adam, 6, 13, 147–148
Adhan (call to prayer), 38
Ahlul Bayt (People of the House), 84, 86, 109
Alcohol, 130–131
Ali (cousin of Muhammad), 69, 72, 75, 77, 80–82, 153
Allah, 3. *See also* God
Almsgiving (zakat), 41–43
Angels, 6, 7–10
Arabic language, 12–13, 34, 91, 100–101
Archangels, 7
Azrael (archangel), 7

B

Banking, 127–128
Battles, 73–74
Bible, 11–12, 140–143

C

Caliphs, 79–81
Calligraphy, 102–103
Celebrations, 47, 131–133
Charity, 41–43
Charter of Madinah, 72, 154
Children, 119–120
Christianity, 11–12, 140–148, 151–154
Converts to Islam, 69–71, 136–137
COVID-19 pandemic, and Shari'a, 115
Creation story, 6–7, 147–148

D

Death, 22, 125–126
Declaration of Faith (shahadah), 30–33
Demographics, xii–xiii, 118
Dietary laws, 128–131, 142
Divine Will, 1, 24–26
Divorce, 123
Djinn, 6
Dress codes, 134–135
Drink, 128–131
Drugs, 130– 131

E

Economics, 127–128
Eid al-Adha, 131–133
Eid al-Fitr, 47, 131–132
Equity, 95
Eve, 6, 147–148
Extremism, religious, 149–151

F

Family, 119–120. *See also* Marriage
Fasting (sawm), 45–48
Fatima (daughter of Muhammad), 65, 69, 81, 84
Festivals, 47, 131–133
Five Pillars
    hajj (Pilgrimage), 48–55
    salat (Daily Prayers), 33–40
    sawm (Fasting), 45–48
    shahadah (Declaration of Faith), 30–33
    zakat (Almsgiving), 41–43
Food, 128–130
Forgetfulness, 20

Forgiveness, **20–22**, **95**

Free will, **26–27**, **105**

G

Gabriel (archangel), **7**, **9–10**, **64–65**, **72**, **90–91**

God

books of, **10–13**, **140–143**

Divine Will of, **24–26**

names of, **1**, **3**

Oneness of, **2–3**, **5**

prophets of, **13–19**, **142**, **144–148**

qualities of, **3–4**

Gospel, **11–12**, **140–143**

Greetings, **1**

H

Hadith, **12**, **19**, **101**, **107**, **109–111**

Hafez, **12**

Hajj (pilgrimage), **48–55**

Halal, **129–130**, **142**

Hanifs, **4**

Hassan (grandson of Muhammad), **66**, **84**

Healing, **13**

Hell, **22–24**

Hijri calendar, **72**

Holidays, **47**, **131–133**

Hope, **95**

Humanity, **96**

Hussein (grandson of Muhammad), **66**, **84**, **86–87**

I

Idols, **4–5**

Ihram (sanctity), **53**

Imams, **114**

Inheritance, **120–121**

Interest, earning, **127–128**

Interfaith movements, **152–153**

Islam, meaning of, **1**

Ismail (prophet), **4**, **51–52**, **132–133**

J

Jesus, **10**, **11–12**, **144–146**

Jihad, **44–45**

Judaism, **11–12**, **140–143**, **151–154**

Judgment Day, **19–24**

Justice, **93–94**

K

Ka'ba, **4–5**, **37**, **48–55**, **59**, **61**

Khadija (wife of Muhammad), **61**, **65–66**, **69**, **124**

al-Khattab, Omar, **70**, **80**

L

Law (Shari'a), **105–106**, **111–115**

Leadership, **79–82**, **114**

M

Madinah, **54**, **71–73**

Marriage, **121–123**

Mecca, **4–5**, **48–55**, **59**, **67–69**

Meccan period, **67–69**

migration to Madinah, **71–73**

revelation of Qur'an by Gabriel, **9–10**, **64–65**, **90–92**

Mercy, **13**, **18–19**, **93**

Messengers, of God, **16–19**. *See also* Prophets

Michael (archangel), **7**

Minorities, religious, **154**

Miracles, **17**

Modesty, **134–135**

Monotheism, **2**, **5**, **10**, **141**, **143**

Moses, **10**, **11–12**

Mosques, **38–39**

Muhammad, Prophet. *See also* Hadith; Sunnah

battles, **73–74**
death of, **75**
family life, **65–66**
as the final prophet, **13**, **18–19**
importance of, **2**
life of, **60–63**
Muslims, defined, **1**

N

Nahj al-Balagha (Ali), **82**
Nature, **95–96**

P

Paganism, pre-Islam, **58–60**
Paradise, **24**
Persecution, **68–69**, **154**
Pilgrimage (hajj), **48–55**
Polygamy, **123–124**
Prayers
    Daily (salat), **33–37**
    on Fridays, **40**
    in mosques, **38–39**
Predestination, **24–27**
Prophets, **4, 10, 13–19, 57–58, 94,**
    142, 144–148
Prostrations, **37**

Q

Qur'an
    angels, **8–9**
    building of Ka'ba, **4**
    chapters of, **90–91**
    creation story, **6–7, 147–148**
    daily use of, **102–103**
    Day of Judgment, **22–24**
    Divine Will, **25–26**
    God as Allah in, **2–3**
    importance of, **92**
    interpretation of, **99–102**
    Jesus in, **144–146**

major themes of, **93–96**
and other holy books, **140–143**
prophets, **13–19**
as revelation, **10–11, 12–13, 89**
revelation of by Gabriel, **9–10,**
    64–65, 90–92
significant verses, **98–99**
Surah Al-Fatiha, **97–98**

R

Ramadan, **45–48, 65**
Ramy (casting stones), **54**
Redemption, **20–21, 148**
Reflection, **94–95**
Revelation, **10–13, 64**

S

Sadaqah (voluntary charity), **43**
as-Salaam (Source of Peace), **1**
Salat (Daily Prayers), **33–40**
Satan, **6, 66–67**
Sawm (fasting), **45–48**
Seal of Prophecy, **18**
Shahadah (Declaration of Faith), **30–33**
Shari'a (law), **105–106, 111–115**
Shi'a school of thought, **77–78, 81–82,**
    84–87, 109
Shrines, **87**
Sin, **20–22, 148**
Sufism, **82–84**
Sunnah, **19, 106–109**
Sunni school of thought, **77–81, 84–87**

T

Tafsirs, **101–102**
Tajwid, art of, **103**
Taqwa (God-consciousness), **26**
Tawhid (Oneness of God), **2**
Timeline, xiv–xv
Tolerance, **154**
Torah, **11–12, 140–143**

U

Ummah (community of believers), **31, 117**
Usury, **127–128**
Uthman bin 'Affan, **80**

V

Violence, **149–151**

W

Women's right, **122, 124–125**

X

X, Malcolm, **50**

Y

Yathrib (Madinah), **71-73**

Z

Zakat (almsgiving), **41-43**

ACKNOWLEDGMENTS

In the dedication of this book, I mentioned *du'a goyān*. This translates to those who supplicate and pray (for self and others). The blessings in my life have been a result of the du'as: the supplications, kindness, and encouragement of those who have remembered me in their prayers and words, who have trusted me with their time, and who have been a part of my journey. I pray that their share of blessings and special grace is magnified. Their beautiful example and warmth reminds me to be of the *du'a goyān*. Life is only experienced through love, love through humbleness, and humbleness through sincerity and the consonance of the inner and the outer. Thank you to all who've taught me this directly and indirectly—and a special thanks to those who've forgiven me when I've failed at this. Alhamdulilah. Allahomma salle 'ala Muhammad wa Āle Muhammad.

ABOUT THE AUTHOR

Ahmad Rashid Salim was born in Kabul, Afghanistan, and raised in the Bay Area. He has studied Islamic sciences both in the context of traditional Islamic learning and in academia. He leads spiritual services in Oakland, lectures and teaches, and is a doctoral student at the University of California, Berkeley.